THE TABLETOP LEARNING SERIES

PRIVATE "I"

The World of Intrigue Begins with You
by Imogene Forte

Incentive Publications, Inc.
Nashville, Tennessee

Illustrated by Gayle Seaberg Harvey
Cover designed by Mary Hamilton and illustrated by Becky Cutler
Edited by Susan Oglander

Library of Congress Catalog Number 84-62933
ISBN 0-86530-096-8

Copyright © 1985 by Incentive Publications, Inc., Nashville, Tennessee. All rights reserved. No part of this publication may be reproduced, stored in a retrieval system, or transmitted in any way or by any means (electronic, mechanical, photocopying, recording, or otherwise) without prior written permission from Incentive Publications, Inc.

THE TABLETOP LEARNING SERIES™ is a trademark of Incentive Publications, Inc., Nashville, TN 37215

THIS PRIVATE "I" BOOK BELONGS TO

_____

CONTENTS

ix   A Note to Kids

ALL EYES ON THE "I"
- 13   Your Fingerprint Is Your Own
- 14   Vita, Please
- 16   Passport Passage
- 18   The Perfect Partner
- 20   What's So Special
- 23   Treasure Your Thoughts
- 24   Is That So
- 26   Detective in Disguise
- 28   Face Value
- 29   Memory Maker, Memory Maker
- 31   Copycat
- 32   A Private Place

GET THE MESSAGE
- 37   Mirror, Mirror on the Wall
- 38   Body Language
- 40   Code It
- 41   Using Invisible Ink
- 42   The Heat Is On
- 43   Message Magic
- 44   A Run-On Message
- 45   Morse Code

46	Make a Map
48	Dial-a-Code
50	Decode the Message
51	Your Turn

NO JOB TOO BIG OR TOO SMALL

55	The Purse Is the Clue
56	A Good Deed a Day
58	Who Did It?
59	Caught in the Act
60	The Better To See You With
62	The Case of the Missing Clocks
66	Put Your Facts Together
67	Lunch Box Snoop
69	Fingerprint Mystery
70	X Marks the Spot
72	They Won't Tell
74	Different People
75	The Secret Is Out
77	In Trouble

A NOTE TO KIDS

With this **Private "I"** book, anyone can learn to be a "cloak-and-dagger" expert! Transport yourself into the world of high intrigue, uncovering secrets and schemes, solving mysteries and decoding messages — all while learning a great deal about yourself and those around you.

First, you'll take a long, hard look at yourself by creating a vita, passport and other essential tools of the trade. You will also examine the talents and abilities you have that will enable you to operate "undercover." Next, the codes and signals will test your creative thinking and problem-solving skills, skills that are so important to your role as a "super sleuth." Finally, once these skills have been mastered, you can become an effective detective, ready to solve the mysteries and secrets that will be the true test of your private "I" abilities.

In any case, hours of fun are in store as you create disguises, discover hide-outs, solve whodunits and much more!

Imogene Forte

ALL EYES ON THE "I"

MY OWN "I"-DEAS

YOUR FINGERPRINT IS YOUR OWN

and no one else's

Your fingerprint is *your* stamp of identity, and no two fingerprints are alike. Even the prints of all your fingers are different. If someone commits a crime and the fingerprints match someone whom the police suspect committed the crime, there will be sufficient proof to prosecute, since no two prints are alike. In order to better understand how detectives use fingerprints in solving crimes, study your own fingerprints. All you will need is a stamp pad, a piece of paper and a magnifying glass for a better look. Press your finger into the stamp pad and then onto the paper. Examine the lines and other identifying marks. Then, look at some of your other fingers and their prints. Compare them to see how they are similar or different.

VITA, PLEASE
or résumé, if you prefer

Vita and résumé are two big words for a summary written by you, about you, to tell folks who you are and what you can do. This can be very important for someone who needs to impress a person whom they cannot talk to in person.

A private "I" certainly needs an impressive vita. So, get some practice in presenting yourself in the very best light with a vita "ready on request."

Use the outline on the following page to get started. Then, add any important talents, abilities, ambitions or other features that make *you* the one-of-a-kind, very special private "I" that you are.

Name

Address

Phone number   Age

Place of birth

Education

Schools

Grade completed

Best subjects

Special abilities

Hobbies

Ambitions

Past mystery-solving experiences

PASSPORT PASSAGE
it identifies only you

To be a true international detective, you will need a passport. A passport allows you to travel in foreign countries and certifies your identity and citizenship. Fill out the information on this passport so you will have all the necessary credentials in case a situation should arise for distant travel.

Be sure to keep your passport in a safe place. It is a document that requires careful handling and attention.

```
→ WARNING: ALTERATION, ADDITION OR MUTILATION OF ENTRIES IS
  PROHIBITED. ANY UNOFFICIAL CHANGE WILL RENDER THIS
  PASSPORT INVALID.
```

NAME -	
SEX -	BIRTHPLACE -
BIRTH DATE -	
WIFE / HUSBAND -	ISSUE DATE -
MINORS - CHILDREN	EXPIRES ON -
	SIGNATURE OF BEARER -

→ IMPORTANT: THIS PASSPORT IS NOT VALID UNTIL SIGNED BY THE BEARER.

ATTACH PHOTOGRAPH HERE

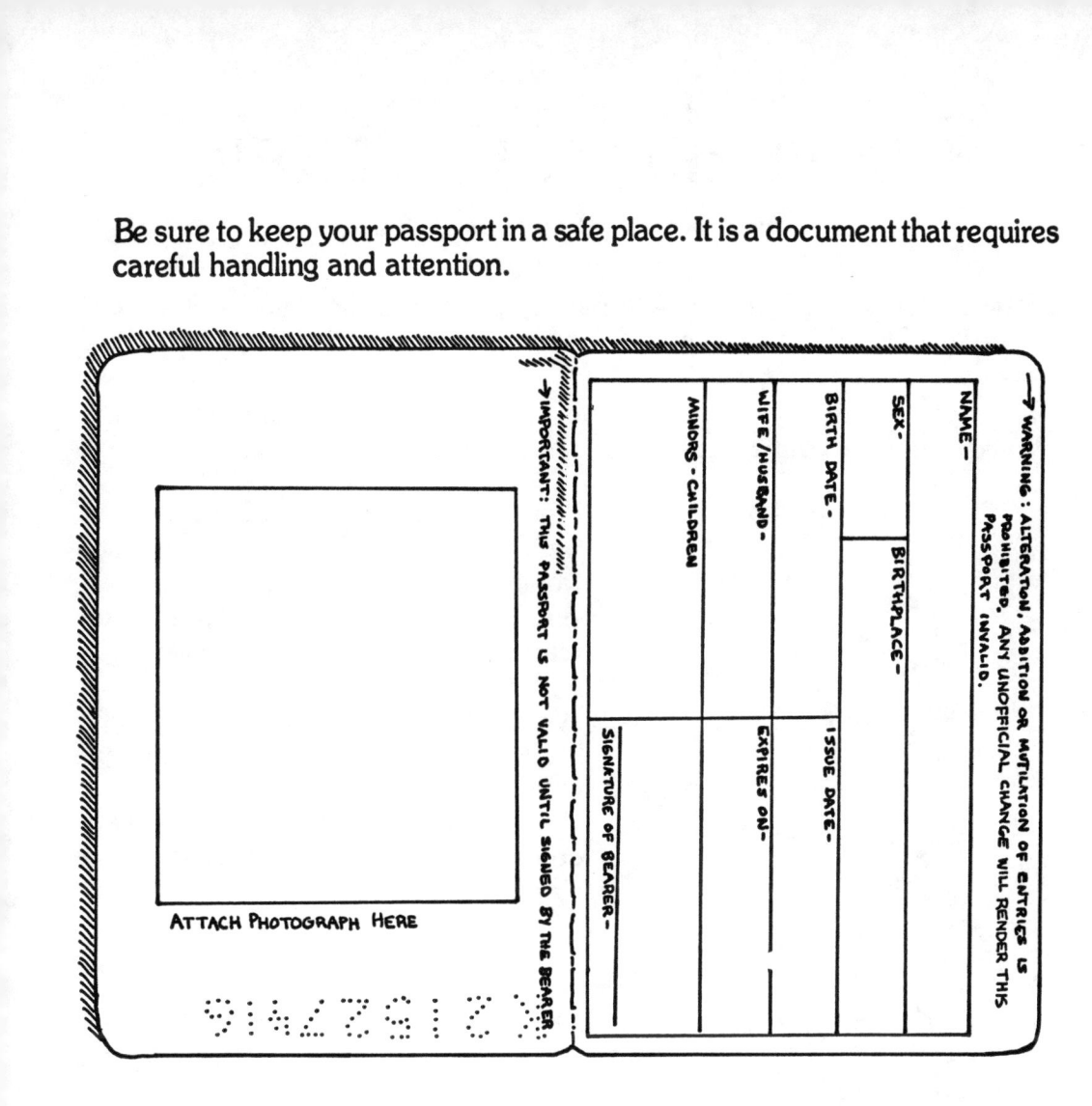

K2152746

THE PERFECT PARTNER
is it too good to be true?

Imagine that you could create a perfect partner to help you solve the mysteries of life. Think about what you would look for in this person.

Would you rather have a boy or a girl for a partner, or does it matter? Would you want your partner to be your age, older or younger?

What interests, hobbies, likes, dislikes (reading, stamp collecting, soccer, etc.) would you want to share?

What special skills or abilities (good reader, fast runner, etc.) would you look for?

What other personal qualities (honesty, loyalty, generosity, etc.) would you want your partner to have?

Where would you want your partner to come from (close by, across town, classmate)?

Consider all of these characteristics and others that occur to you. Write your own description of the "perfect partner."

Now, think about all the people you know and select the person who comes closest to being the "perfect partner" for you.

WHAT'S SO SPECIAL
about the people you know?

Not everyone will be the "perfect partner" for you, but every human being is special in some way.

> Some are short, others are tall,
> Some are fat, others are small,
> Some talk a lot, others are quiet,
> Some run fast, others are slow and steady,
> Some wait around, others are always ready,
> Some read, others hate books,
> Some play games, others prefer work.

The list could go on and on, but the bottom line is we are all different and special in our own way.

It takes a very good private "I" to find out the special things about people. This project will go a long way to prepare you for the world of special investigation.

You will need 5" x 7" index cards and a couple of well-sharpened pencils. Write the names of five classmates or family members at the top of the cards (one name per card).

```
Name                    Date
Address
Birthday                Weight
Hobbies
Likes                   Dislikes



Something special


```

Interview each person and carefully record the data on your interview card. When you have finished, look carefully at your cards. Did you learn some things about each person that you didn't know before? Does some of the information surprise you? Finding out things you never knew before or might never have known, is one of the special bonuses of becoming a very special private "I".

TREASURE YOUR THOUGHTS
they're yours alone

You know, your own thoughts and ideas are real treasures, too. They are uniquely *yours*, so that makes them very special. A private "I" must be able to think clearly and come up with good ideas and well-thought-out plans. Make a list of some of your own thoughts and ideas that you "treasure." It will help you with your "detecting" abilities.

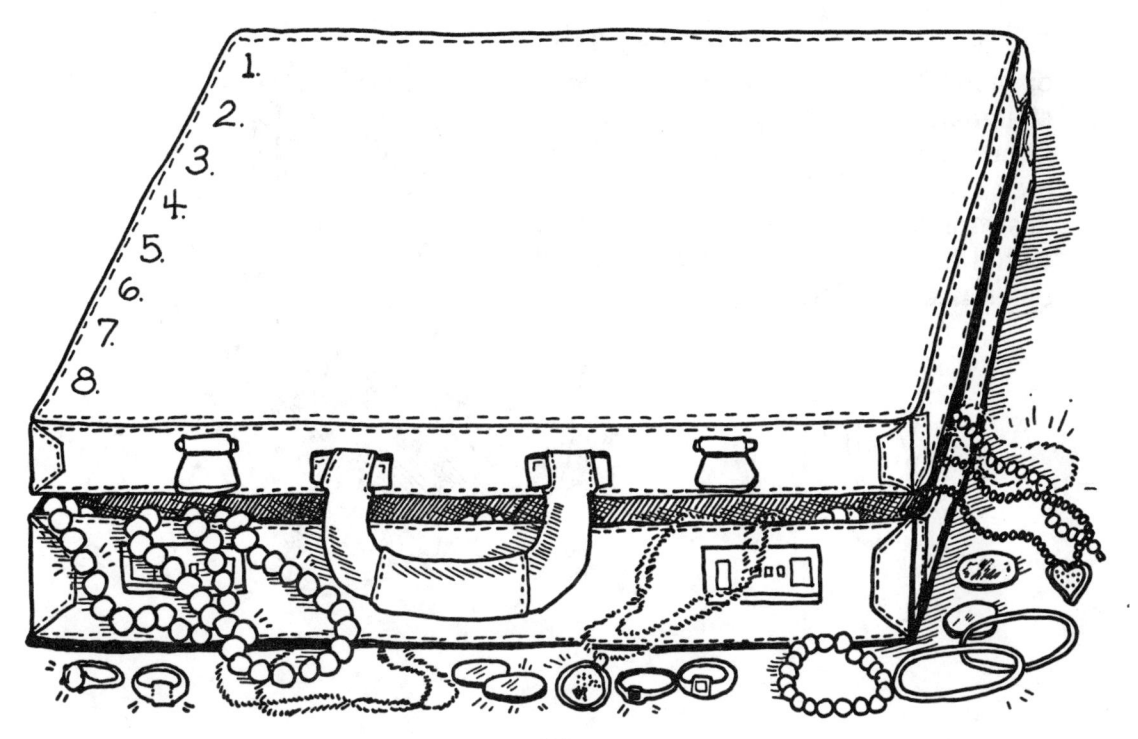

1.
2.
3.
4.
5.
6.
7.
8.

IS THAT SO

or do you just think so?

Being able to determine the difference between fact and opinion has helped to solve many mysteries.

It's easy to fall into the habit of believing everything you hear or thinking that everything you read is absolutely true. This can be particularly dangerous because some news is reported before all the facts are in.

Check your ability to tell fact from opinion by writing **F** before each statement that you believe is a fact and **O** beside the statements that you think are opinions. Think carefully before answering, then discuss the statements with a friend to see if indeed there is a difference of opinion.

_____ This is the coldest January we have had in years.

_____ Teachers are always kind people.

_____ There are 50 states in the United States, and the last state to be admitted to the Union was Hawaii.

_____ If the groundhog sees his shadow when he comes out of his hole on February 2nd, more cold weather is on the way.

_____ Jupiter is the largest planet in our solar system.

_____ The largest continent is Asia and the second largest is Africa.

_____ Cats make better pets than dogs.

_____ Boys can jump higher than girls.

DETECTIVE IN DISGUISE
so you won't be recognized

The time will surely come when you will need to disguise yourself in order to snoop around in places where you might be recognized. First, you will need to decide what kind of character you want to be — a cowboy, chef, hobo, glamour queen or something in between? This is your chance to pretend to be anything or anybody you want to be. Now, begin to put your disguise together.

You will want to organize your clothes. To make it simple, you can use your own clothes and add patches, stripes, long skirts or fancy pants. Or, maybe a long coat that belongs to a tall person in your family would be the perfect "cover-up." The important thing is to design your outfit so you can be in complete disguise in a matter of minutes.

Wigs are fun to make and even more fun to wear. You could use an old one that someone you know is ready to discard, or make your own from a paper bag. To make a paper bag wig, just cut the bag to fit your head, cut fringe and roll the fringe around a pencil to curl it. You can make long hair or short hair, bangs, a ponytail or you can use cotton, string or yarn for a more dramatic effect. Or, how about a mop top?

FACE VALUE
to hide your true identity

Now, it's time for the face. Will you need a beard, mustache, long eyelashes, eyeglasses, a big nose or funny teeth? Some of these things can be purchased inexpensively at five-and-dime stores, others you will need to make. Try making a beard from cotton, long eyelashes cut from construction paper, a mustache from an old wig or whatever else you can think of. Let your imagination run wild and your face will show just how creative you are.

MEMORY MAKER, MEMORY MAKER

make me a memory

For a private "I," a good memory is a must! In spite of what you may have been told, you can train yourself to remember more. Like many things, it just takes practice. You begin by looking at people, places and things more carefully and trying to fix the details of what you see in your mind. Once you get in the habit of "looking to remember," it gets easier all the time. Test yourself right now on how carefully you have been looking at the world around you. Give yourself 5 points for every question you can answer with "yes." Total your score. If you have a score of 50 or more, you are on your way to becoming a "memory maker." If not, you need to begin working on it right now.

____ Can you describe in detail the clothing the first person you saw today was wearing?
____ Can you list every single food you ate yesterday?
____ Do you remember exactly what time you got up and what time you went to bed yesterday?
____ Can you name every person who spoke to you yesterday?
____ Do you know how many kids are in your school?
____ Can you tell how many clocks are in your house?
____ Do you know exactly how old your parents are and the dates of their birthdays?
____ Do you know what color your teacher's hair and eyes are?
____ Do you know how many pieces of mail were delivered to your house yesterday?
____ Do you know who baked the last birthday cake you helped to eat?
____ Do you know how many pages were in the last book you read?
____ Do you know how many pairs of socks you own?

COPYCAT

a true memory test

Test your memory again by trying this copycat test.

Look at the figures in the box below for two minutes. Cover the page with another piece of paper and try to draw the figures exactly as you remember them. Check your work to see how well you did. Then, make a copycat test for a friend and see how well he does.

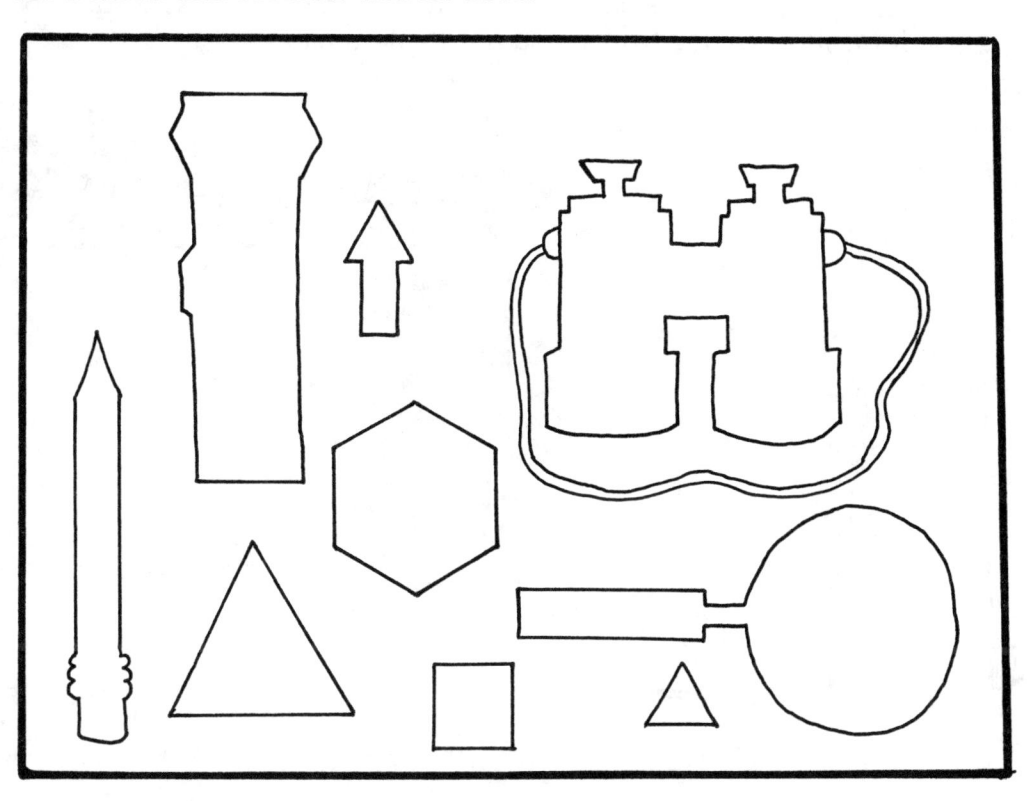

A PRIVATE PLACE
if you please

Every private "I" needs a private place, a place to go to think about the good things that are happening, or when things are not going so well, to think about how to make things better. Sometimes a private "I" just needs to be alone for awhile, maybe to rest and not think at all.

Do you have a private place of your own? If you don't, look around for a place that will be just right for you. Check to be sure your secret place is safe and meets with the grownups' approval. Make yourself a sign that says:

Private Please

You will be all set to hang your sign out the next time you want to be alone in your own special hideaway for awhile.

GET THE MESSAGE

MY OWN "I"-DEAS

MIRROR, MIRROR ON THE WALL
can you read this message at all?

Write a secret message backward. Time your partner to see how long it takes to read it with the help of a mirror. Keep working at it until you both get faster and faster at mirror reading.

BODY LANGUAGE
actions speak louder than words

While you are working with the mirror, you and your partner may want to practice copying each other in action.

To begin, one of you should stand close to a mirror, with the other person standing a few feet behind. Both partners should be looking directly into the mirror and be able to see each other's actions clearly.

The acting partner makes all kinds of different movements for the other partner to copy *exactly*. Movements could include touching the right hand to the top of the head, the left hand to the right knee, both hands crossed over the chest, clapping, winking one eye then the other, sticking out the tongue, etc.

Take turns being the actor or the follower, then get ready to send some *real* messages.

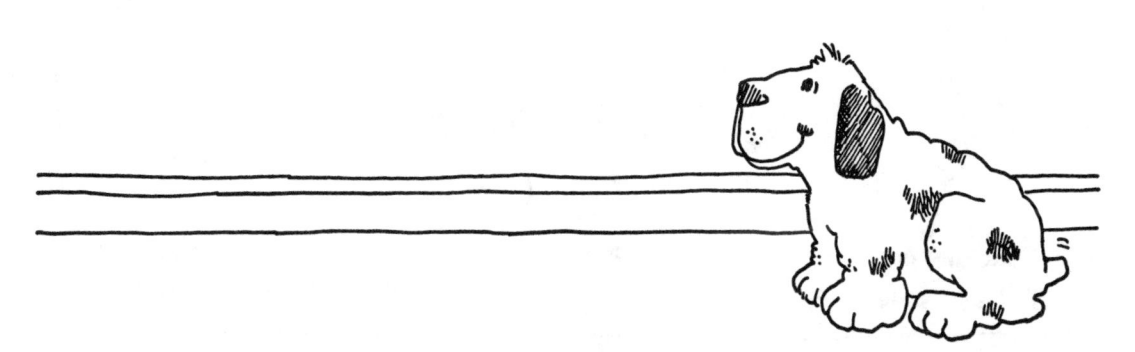

CODE IT
give real meaning to actions

Make up an action code and use it when you need to send top-secret messages without making a sound.

Maybe some of these will help you get started.

Arms over chest in X, DANGER!

Pointing, right, left, in front, behind, giving directions.

Finger on lips, quiet, not a word!

Waving the hand, goodbye!

Touching ear, I hear something!

Hands outstretched, "flopping" RUN!

Touching nose, I smell something!

USING INVISIBLE INK
it's easier than you think

There's more than one way to send a message that only the person who holds *your* secret will be able to read. Try using several of these "invisible inks" to find out which works the best for you. You can use vinegar, lemon or apple juice, or baking soda, sugar and salt dissolved in water. They are all used in the same way. You will need to use paper with a sort of soft or porous surface (newsprint and paper towels are good) and either a small brush or Q-tips to "write" with (your fingers will work in an emergency).

Write your message, let it dry completely and roll it up and tie it with a piece of string. Try some other things too, just to see if they work. Then, the heat is on to read the message!

THE HEAT IS ON
and the message is clear

To read the "invisible ink" message, the receiver will need to hold it before a heat source. This can be done by carefully holding the paper in front of a light bulb. The paper will need to be passed back and forth over the heat source until the words begin to turn brown and "pop right off the paper."

Don't be discouraged if this whole thing doesn't work the first time. Remember, nobody ever said being a private "I" was easy. But isn't it a lot of fun?

MESSAGE MAGIC
write 'em down and go to town

Begin now to make your own list of ways to send and receive secret messages. Try out each one and practice with a partner to make sure that your own "tried-and-true" messages will be at your finger tips when you need them. You will be surprised how fast your list will grow as you think of new and different ways to send your secret messages.

A RUN-ON MESSAGE
you figure out the real meaning

This message can be decoded by separating it into sentences and capitalizing and punctuating where necessary. Work this out, then write a run-on message of your own for a friend to decode.

All good detectives must be alert and industrious lazy people will never make the grade good detectives also need a sense of humor and respect for other people they can not be careless or do poor work because that might cause someone to get hurt learning to stop look and listen and to follow up on clues promptly is the most important thing a detective has to do it is not easy but it sure does make life interesting because people do the funniest things

MORSE CODE
dots and dashes make it happen

Here is a code that is recognized by people all over the world.

A	.-	J	.---	S	...	2	..---
B	-...	K	-.-	T	-	3	...--
C	-.-.	L	.-..	U	..-	4	....-
D	-..	M	--	V	...-	5	.....
E	.	N	-.	W	.--	6	-....
F	..-.	O	---	X	-..-	7	--...
G	--.	P	.--.	Y	-.--	8	---..
H	....	Q	--.-	Z	--..	9	----.
I	..	R	.-.	1	.----	0	-----

Study it and practice sending some messages in Morse code. Then, you too will be prepared to be an international sleuth.

45

MAKE A MAP
and give it to a friend

Every good private "I" knows how important it is to be able to hide and protect valuable information or possessions. Get some practice now so you will be able to stash things away safely when necessary.

Write a secret message to a friend. Roll the message up and put it in a cookie tin or potato chip can. Bury (or hide) your message in a safe place, not *too* hard to find. Make a map for your friend to use and watch to see how long it takes for your message to be found.

Remember, you can make many different kinds of maps. One might be pictorial and just contain drawings of trees, water, trails, etc. Another might have specific directions using north, south, east and west. And, you could also write out the instructions for reaching the secret message —

take four steps from your house and turn right, etc. In any case, the map needs to be clear and easy to understand. You don't want to have your friend searching for the message for too long, do you?

DIAL-A-CODE
for special secret messages

WHAT TO USE:
- paper plate
- paper fastener
- construction paper
- felt tip pen

WHAT TO DO:
1. Use the felt tip pen to write the letters of the alphabet and the numerals 1-26 on the paper plate to make a Dial-a-Code wheel similar to the one on the following page.
2. Make an arrow from construction paper.
3. Use the paper fastener to hold the arrow in the center of the paper plate.

Now you have a quick and easy code to use to exchange messages with a fellow sleuth.

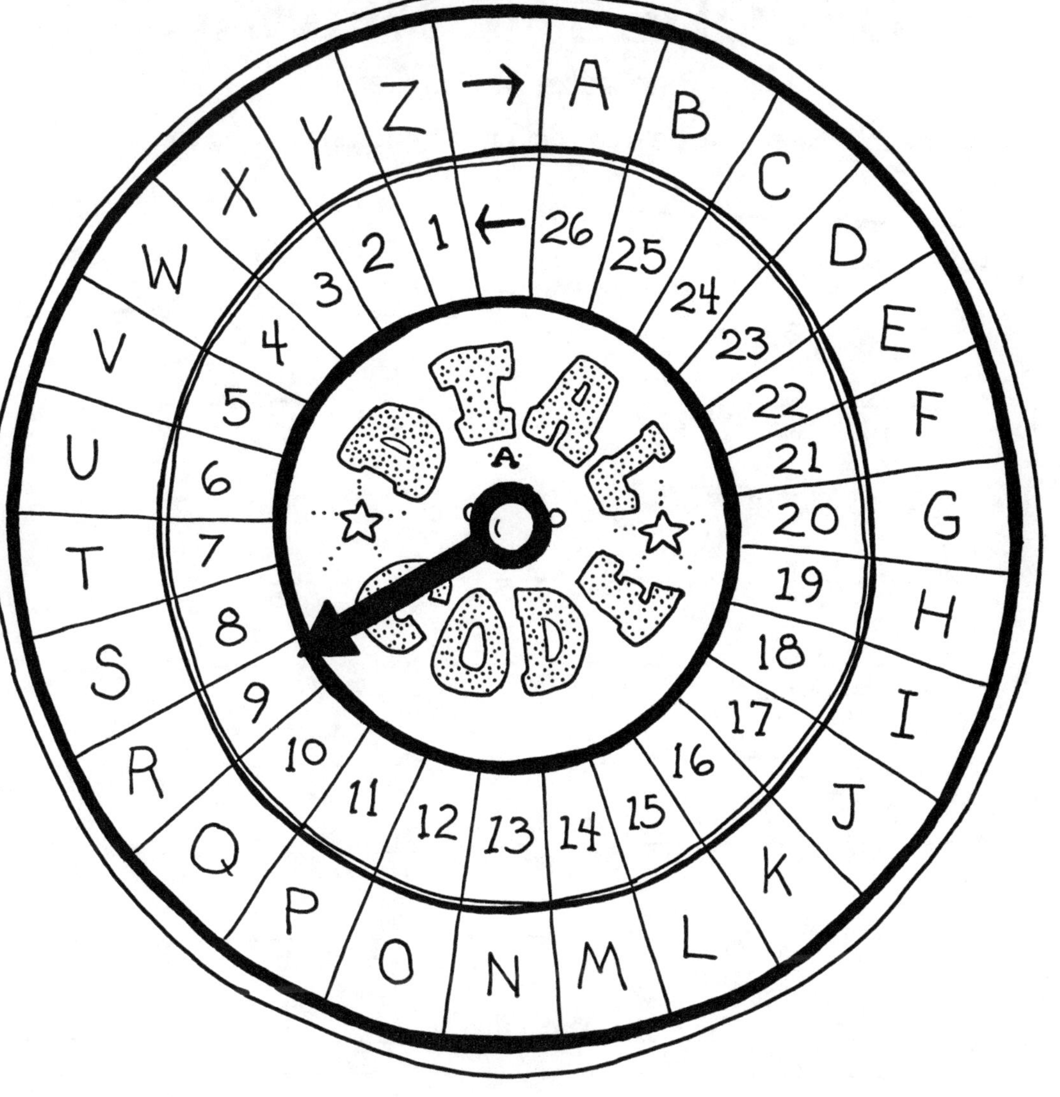

A
B
C
D
E
F
G
H
I
J
K
L
M
N
O
P
Q
R
S
T
U
V
W
X
Y
Z
1
2
3
4
5
6
7
8
9
10
11
12
13
14
15
16
17
18
19
20
21
22
23
24
25
26
DIAL CODE
A

DECODE THE MESSAGE
and solve the mystery

Decode this message to help you get off to a good start using your Dial-a-Code.

$\overline{14}\ \overline{22}\ \overline{22}\ \overline{7}\quad \overline{14}\ \overline{22}\quad \overline{26}\ \overline{21}\ \overline{7}\ \overline{22}\ \overline{9}$

$\overline{8}\ \overline{6}\ \overline{11}\ \overline{11}\ \overline{22}\ \overline{9}\quad \overline{7}\ \overline{12}\ \overline{13}\ \overline{18}\ \overline{20}\ \overline{19}\ \overline{7}$

$\overline{26}\ \overline{7}\quad \overline{12}\ \overline{6}\ \overline{9}\quad \overline{6}\ \overline{8}\ \overline{6}\ \overline{26}\ \overline{15}\quad \overline{14}\ \overline{22}\ \overline{22}\ \overline{7}$

$\overline{18}\ \overline{13}\ \overline{20}\quad \overline{11}\ \overline{15}\ \overline{26}\ \overline{24}\ \overline{22}.\quad \overline{25}\ \overline{9}\quad \overline{18}\ \overline{13}\ \overline{20}$

$\overline{7}\ \overline{19}\ \overline{22}\quad \overline{11}\ \overline{15}\ \overline{26}\ \overline{13}\ \overline{8}\quad \overline{4}\ \overline{18}\ \overline{7}\ \overline{19}\quad \overline{2}\ \overline{12}\ \overline{6}.$

$\overline{26}\ \overline{21}\ \overline{7}\ \overline{22}\ \overline{9}\quad \overline{26}\ \overline{15}\ \overline{15}\quad \overline{7}\ \overline{19}\ \overline{18}\ \overline{8}\quad \overline{7}\ \overline{18}\ \overline{14}\ \overline{22},$

$\overline{18}\ \overline{7}\quad \overline{15}\ \overline{12}\ \overline{12}\ \overline{16}\ \overline{8}\quad \overline{26}\ \overline{8}\quad \overline{18}\ \overline{21}\quad \overline{12}\ \overline{6}\ \overline{9}$

$\overline{25}\ \overline{18}\ \overline{20}\quad \overline{24}\ \overline{26}\ \overline{8}\ \overline{22}\quad \overline{18}\ \overline{8}\quad \overline{26}\ \overline{25}\ \overline{12}\ \overline{6}\ \overline{7}\quad \overline{7}\ \overline{12}$

$\overline{25}\ \overline{9}\ \overline{22}\ \overline{26}\ \overline{16}.\quad \overline{4}\ \overline{22}\quad \overline{14}\ \overline{26}\ \overline{2}\quad \overline{25}\ \overline{22}\quad \overline{19}\ \overline{22}\ \overline{9}\ \overline{12}\ \overline{22}\ \overline{8}!$

50

YOUR TURN
to write one of your own

Select one of these messages to send in code and use the Dial-a-Code to help you write the message.

- Send a Halloween party invitation.
- Ask to borrow a book of spy stories.
- Tell about a visit to a haunted house.
- Report a strange sight you saw.
- Write some jokes.
- Send a message to a person on another planet.

NO JOB TOO BIG OR TOO SMALL

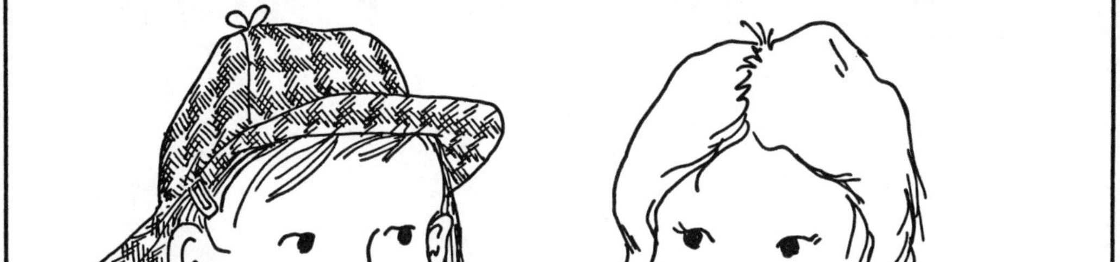

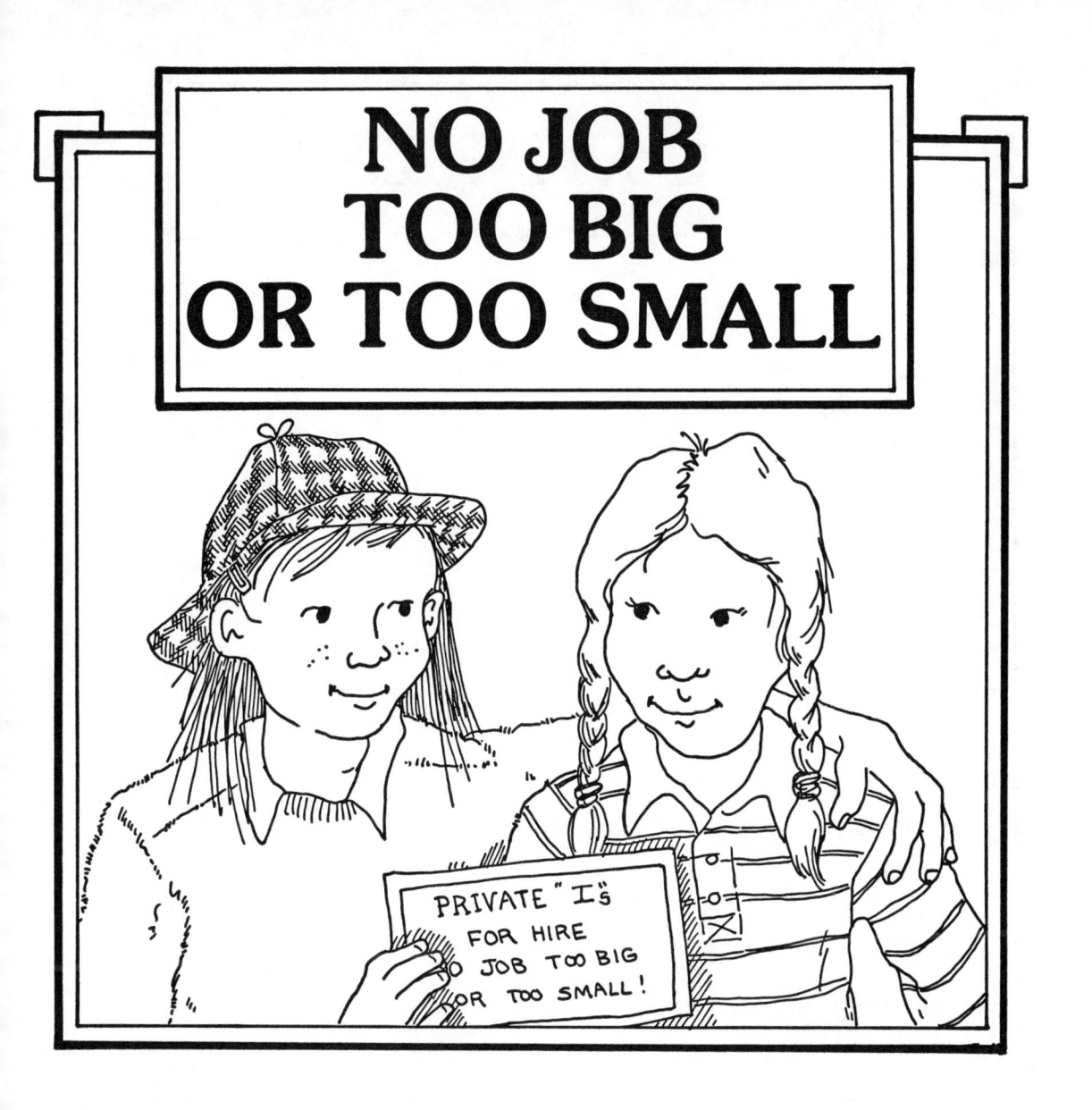

MY OWN "I"-DEAS

THE PURSE IS THE CLUE
whose is it?

Test a friend's detective abilities by making up a small mystery to be solved.

Fill an old purse or briefcase with objects that reflect a certain personality. Maybe you could use a lot of makeup, combs, jewelry, address book, etc., that would indicate one person's interests; a pipe, paperback detective story, money clip, pocket magnifying glass, etc., to show a different personality; or a pair of glasses, pad and pencil, dictionary, apple, etc., to show another.

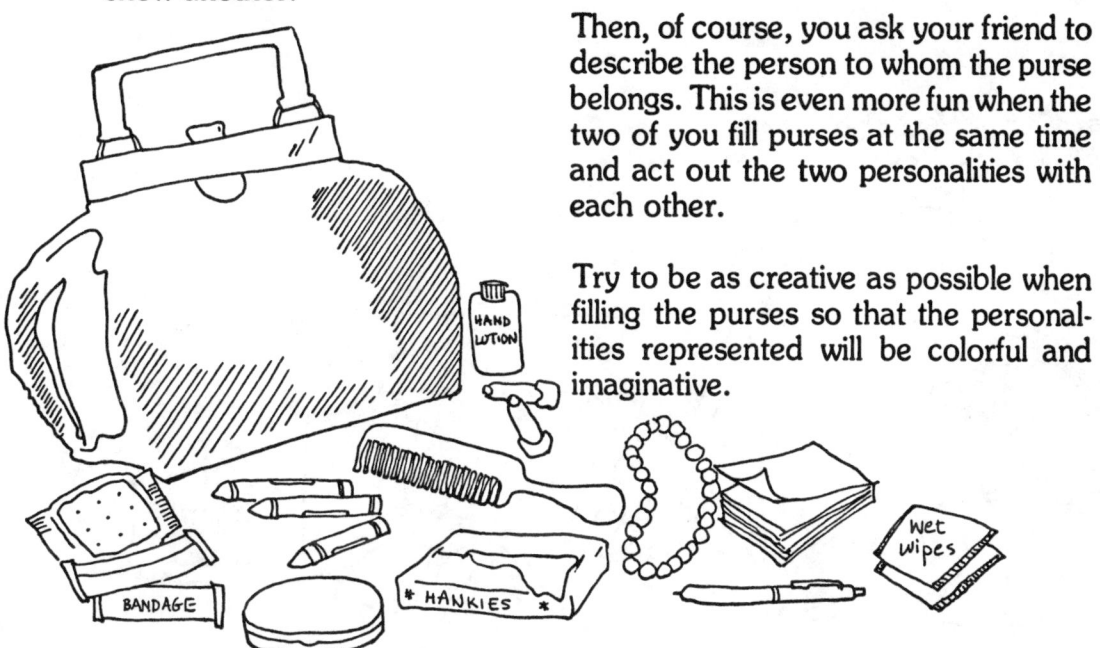

Then, of course, you ask your friend to describe the person to whom the purse belongs. This is even more fun when the two of you fill purses at the same time and act out the two personalities with each other.

Try to be as creative as possible when filling the purses so that the personalities represented will be colorful and imaginative.

A GOOD DEED A DAY
will find friends on the way

Pick out one person in your family, your neighborhood or your classroom to receive a daily good deed for a week — a *secret* good deed, mind you.

Observe the person carefully and plan deeds that are sure to please. To do this, you will need to discover the habits, likes, dislikes and what brings happiness to the person who will receive your good deeds. Maybe one day you could leave flowers or a bunch of beautiful autumn leaves beside the door. Another day, try a small bag of hard candies, a nice note or some jokes. Once you get started, good deeds will come easy.

The fun part of this secret activity will be in watching the person to see how much pleasure your actions bring, and to see how long it takes the person to find out that you are responsible for them!

WHO DID IT?

see if you can find the culprit

Select the person from the lineup that you think committed each of the crimes on the following page. Write a number under each person to match the crime with its "perpetrator."

CAUGHT IN THE ACT

you solve the case

Each of the people shown on the previous page was caught committing one of these misdemeanors.

1. One stole the cookies from the cookie jar.
2. One tied the tin can to the dog's tail.
3. One pulled the baby's hair when no one else was in the room.
4. One skipped school on the first day of spring to go fishing.

Can you tell what happened and how each person was "caught in the act?"

Make up your own versions for these whodunits.

THE BETTER TO SEE YOU WITH

my dear

Make yourself a pair of special binoculars to bring the world into better focus.

WHAT TO USE:
- 2 empty bathroom tissue rolls
- sturdy string
- scissors
- masking tape

WHAT TO DO:
1. Place the tubes flat on a table and hold them together tightly with one hand while you wrap masking tape around both tubes with the other hand. Use plenty of tape to hold the tubes together for "rugged" use.
2. Use the scissors to punch a hole on the top outside edge of each roll.
3. Push one end of the string through each hole to form a neck strap for your binoculars.

4. Knot the end to hold it firmly in place.
5. If you have the time and the paint, give the binoculars a coat of black paint. This will make them look more "professional."

While they are only make-believe binoculars, they really will help you "see" things a little more clearly simply because you will be concentrating on what you see through the two "openings."

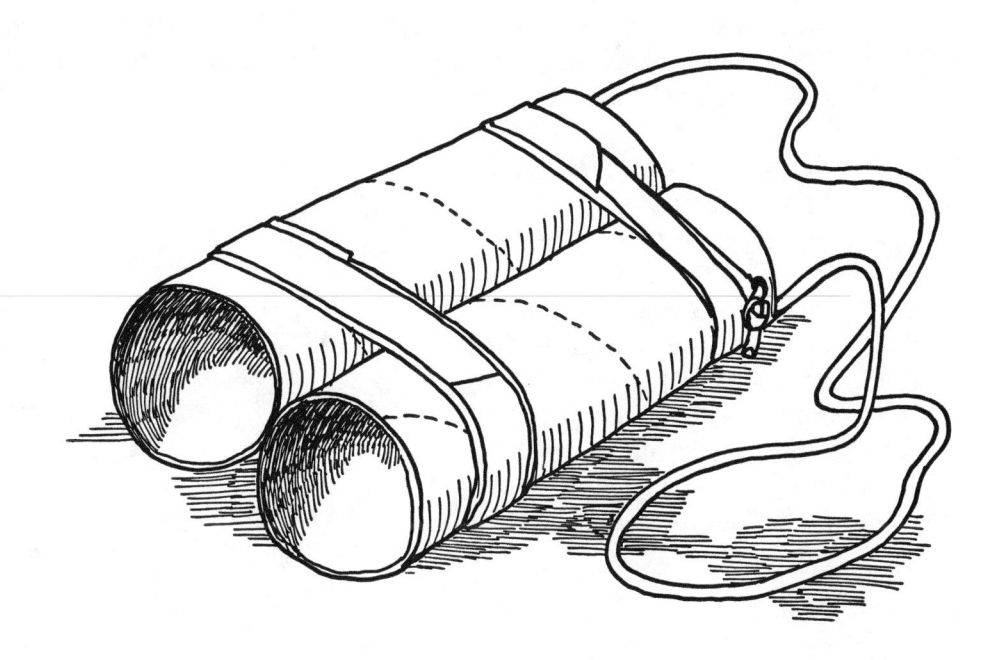

THE CASE OF THE MISSING CLOCKS
someone had the time to do it

Can you solve this mystery? Read the story below and use all your acquired detective skills to find out who took the clocks and why, where the clocks are now and how soon they can be returned to their places in the school.

It was high noon on the last day of summer vacation when something very mysterious was discovered by the principal at the Front Street School. Someone had removed every clock in the entire school! The principal was ready to leave the school after completing a final check to make sure everything was in tiptop shape for the first day of the new school year. She glanced up to check the time on the office wall clock and a bare spot greeted her eyes. She immediately searched the school to find that every single clock was missing — the big clock in the entrance hall, the cafeteria clock, all the clocks in the classrooms and even the tiny clock on the secretary's desk.

The principal called in the police, and together they began to piece together clues in the case of the missing clocks. Who had been in the building that day and what would the motive be for removing all the clocks? Where were the clocks now and how could they be found and replaced before tomorrow?

The school library had been open for last minute book returns, and the principal wanted to question the librarian. The librarian said a group of older kids belonging to a secret club had been very angry because they had been fined for overdue books. As they left the library, he overheard the president of the club say, "This is a stupid school. They'll be sorry for the way they're treating us." The librarian insisted that the kids were not troublemakers; they were just upset about the fines.

The custodian reported that a repair crew had been working on the heating system. He said two of the three repairmen had worked hard and cheerfully all day, while the third one had been grumpy and made frequent trips to and from the van, often carrying his tool kit and other items with him.

The custodian said all three repairmen had worked at the school before, however, and had never appeared to be dishonest.

A Cub Scout troop had met at the school for their last meeting of the summer. The group was unusually loud and unruly, and the leader had finally dismissed the meeting early. He told them to go home, think about their behavior and come to the next meeting with a different attitude. After the troop had left the building, they sat around under the big tree on the lawn telling jokes and singing songs. The leader said they were still there when he left. He was quick to say, however, that these Cub Scouts were honest and trustworthy. He said they were acting silly because they hated to see the vacation end, but they would never commit a crime.

Now, you have all the clues. Use the fact sheet on the following page to build your case. (The fact sheet can be used to help you solve other mysteries, too!) Ask a friend to try to solve the mystery at the same time. Compare your solutions to find out who is the most thorough private "I."

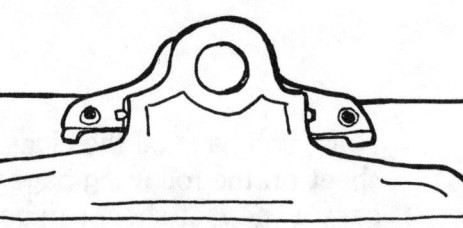

PUT YOUR FACTS TOGETHER
and figure it out

Suspects: Secret Club, Repair Crew, Cub Scouts

Motives: Secret Club _____

            Repair Crew _____

            Cub Scouts _____

Clues from interviews _____
_____
_____

Witnesses _____

Final suspects _____

Who did it? _____
Why? _____

The answer is up to you. Pretend to question your sources and collect clues after you have listed suspects and motives. Carefully look over all your information and decide who you think the culprits are.

LUNCH BOX SNOOP
after a big scoop

What can you tell about people from what they eat or throw away?

Some kids eat greens, fresh fruits and nuts, while others stuff their bodies with lots of junk food. It may not always be chubby Chip who does away with a whole cake and three peanut butter sandwiches at one sitting. Sometimes tiny Tim is the unsuspected glutton. And, you just might be surprised by what one person considers a balanced lunch and another looks at as just a snack. Some picky kids eat only part of their food and the rest goes in the garbage. Other, more conservation-conscious kids, plan ahead and bring foods they know they will eat.

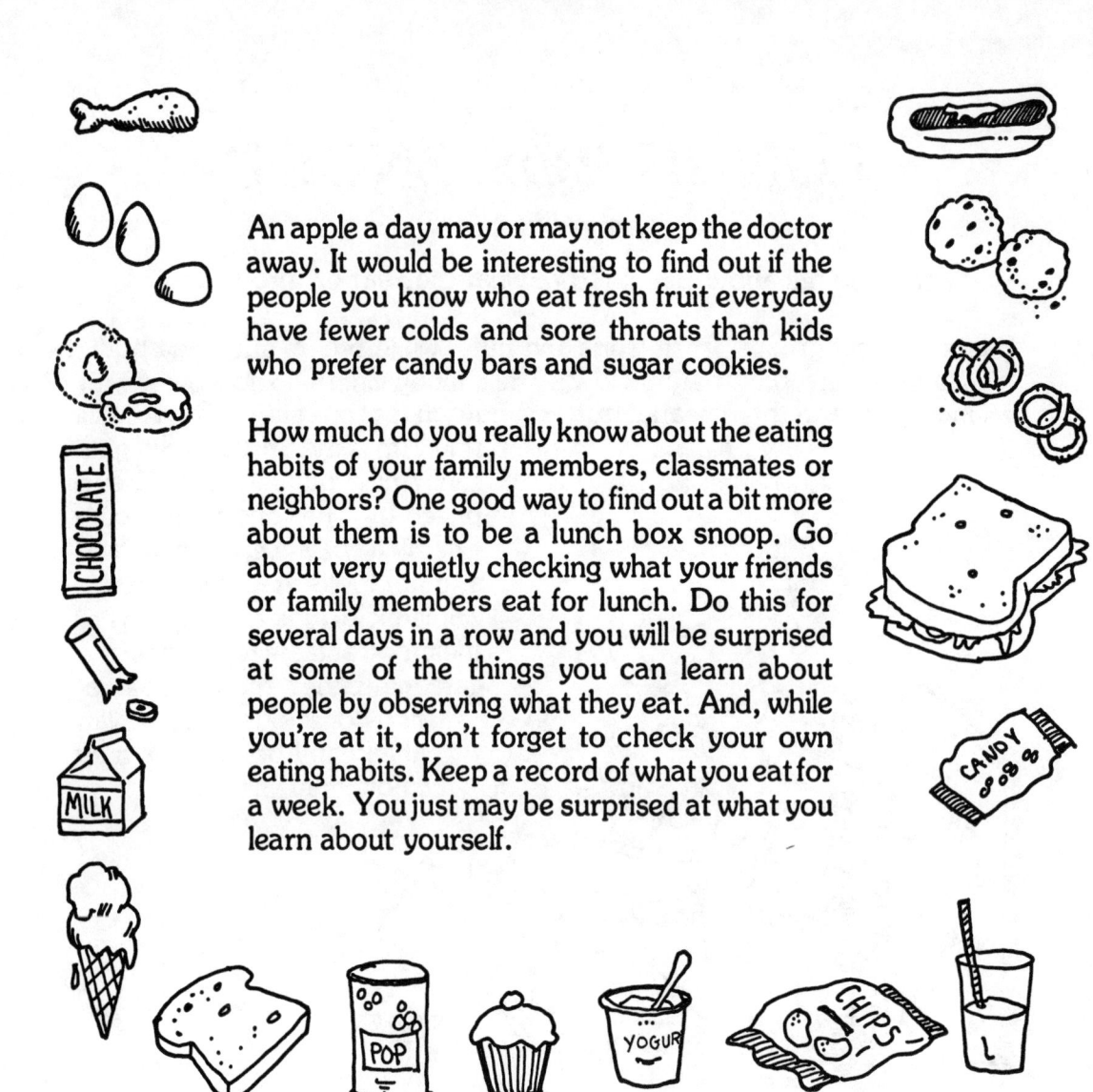

An apple a day may or may not keep the doctor away. It would be interesting to find out if the people you know who eat fresh fruit everyday have fewer colds and sore throats than kids who prefer candy bars and sugar cookies.

How much do you really know about the eating habits of your family members, classmates or neighbors? One good way to find out a bit more about them is to be a lunch box snoop. Go about very quietly checking what your friends or family members eat for lunch. Do this for several days in a row and you will be surprised at some of the things you can learn about people by observing what they eat. And, while you're at it, don't forget to check your own eating habits. Keep a record of what you eat for a week. You just may be surprised at what you learn about yourself.

FINGERPRINT MYSTERY
innocent or guilty?

For a different twist with your fingerprints, you can make lots of characters as part of a mystery story. Try funny people, animals or even interesting aliens. Present the story to your friends and let them figure out whodunit.

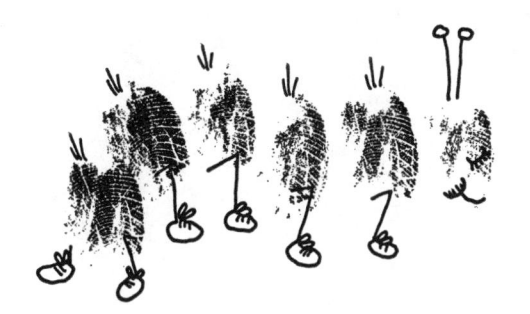

Did the innocent mouse do it, or was it the clown on the corner with the balloons?

X MARKS THE SPOT
to lead to a special treasure

Here's a way to have some fun with trail markings. Leave a trail for a friend leading to a special treasure. It could be a book, some candy or a favorite drawing. Here are some suggestions for markers.

- three leaves with a stick through the center
- some acorns gathered in a pile
- branches stacked in an interesting way
- rocks laid in the shape of an arrow pointing a certain direction

Make up other trail markings and let your friend try to follow them to the special treasure. You can give your friend a list so she will have a reference to go by. Then, let your friend make up one for you. Happy trails!

THEY WON'T TELL
who will?

Something very strange has happened and all of these people know about it. They are not talking, however, and it is up to you as a private "I" to find out what their secret is. You have very few clues to go on, so you will have to be very sharp and use all your "super snooper" techniques to solve this one.

THESE PEOPLE HAVE A SECRET. CAN YOU GUESS WHAT IT IS?

Here are the clues ...

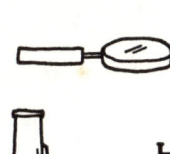

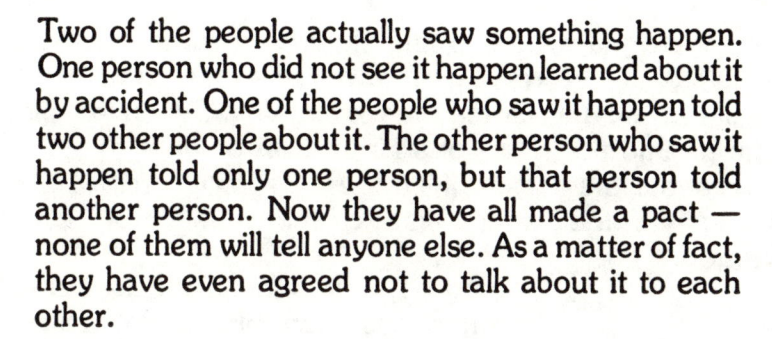

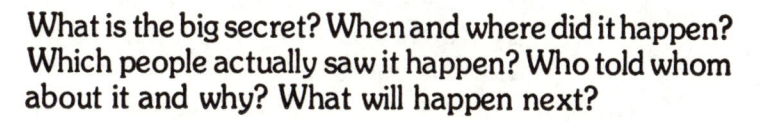

Two of the people actually saw something happen. One person who did not see it happen learned about it by accident. One of the people who saw it happen told two other people about it. The other person who saw it happen told only one person, but that person told another person. Now they have all made a pact — none of them will tell anyone else. As a matter of fact, they have even agreed not to talk about it to each other.

What is the big secret? When and where did it happen? Which people actually saw it happen? Who told whom about it and why? What will happen next?

Write or tell someone about the secret. It would be fun to ask a friend to do this with you to see how different your versions of the secret are.

DIFFERENT PEOPLE

a different mystery

Now, it is your turn.

Look through old magazines to find pictures of some interesting-looking people to involve in a secret of your own. Look for pictures of people with interesting faces and unusual features or clothing. Cut out the pictures and paste them around the edges of a large sheet of writing paper. Print the instructions about the secret which these people share at the top of the paper. Try to make the instructions as clear as possible, but leave some air of mystery, too.

Give the paper to a friend and ask her to find the secret. This is a fun thing to do on a rainy afternoon. All you need is a friend, a big stack of old magazines, scissors, glue, paper and pencils and a vivid imagination.

THE SECRET IS OUT
but who knows?

One more way to have fun with this secret activity is to turn it around and start from the other end. Every private "I" has to be able to go about problem-solving in many different ways, you know.

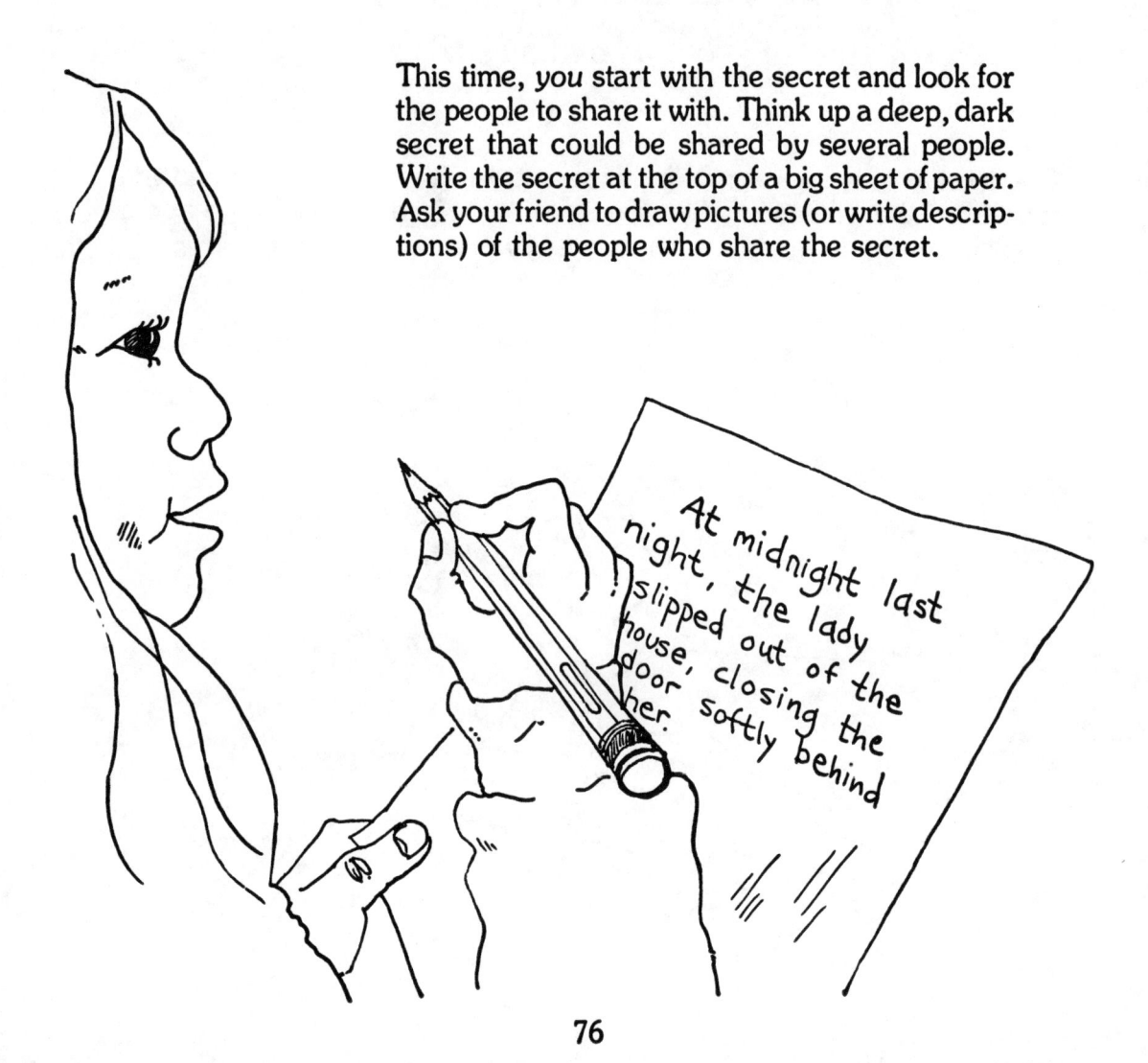

This time, you start with the secret and look for the people to share it with. Think up a deep, dark secret that could be shared by several people. Write the secret at the top of a big sheet of paper. Ask your friend to draw pictures (or write descriptions) of the people who share the secret.

At midnight last night, the lady slipped out of the house, closing the door softly behind her.

IN TROUBLE
out of trouble

How good are you at figuring out how to get yourself out of a tight spot? Think about each of the situations below and plot a strategy you would use to free yourself.

You awake to find yourself still in your pajamas, in a strange, brightly lit room surrounded by giants. You have no idea who brought you here and why. Even though the giants look friendly enough, your first thought is how to get out of the room and back home. You can see that the door is locked and the only window is closed. What will your first move be?

You and your best friend are enjoying a picnic in the park when a huge rhinoceros comes charging out of the woods and stands glaring at you. You can't remember if a rhinoceros is a friendly animal, so you are not sure what to do. Meanwhile, your friend becomes very frightened and begins to yell at the top of her lungs. The rhinoceros appears to be angry about the yelling and is giving you threatening looks, which causes your friend to become more frightened and to yell even louder. The situation does not look very good. What will you do now?

Oh no! It's midnight on a stormy Halloween night. The two beady eyes you see looking into your bedroom window do not look friendly at all. You try to cry out for help, but your voice simply won't work. The window is slowly being raised. A huge, hairy paw is poking through and the beady eyes are directly on you. What in the world can you do?

pilgrim

A COURSE FOR THE CHRISTIAN JOURNEY
THE EUCHARIST

STEPHEN COTTRELL
STEVEN CROFT
PAULA GOODER
ROBERT ATWELL

Contributions from
ANGELA TILBY   SIMON JONES
JOHN PRITCHARD   JOHN INGE

THE CHURCH OF ENGLAND

CHURCH HOUSE PUBLISHING

Church House Publishing
Church House
Great Smith Street
London SW1P 3AZ

ISBN 9780 7151 4447 3

Published 2014 by Church House Publishing

Third impression 2017

Copyright © 2014 Stephen Cottrell, Steven Croft, Robert Atwell and Paula Gooder

Cover image – Bread image: Syrota Vadym/Shutterstock.com
Under license from Shutterstock.com

All rights reserved. No part of this publication may be reproduced or stored or transmitted by any means or in any form, electronic or mechanical, including photocopying, recording, or any information storage and retrieval system without written permission, which should be sought from copyright@churchofengland.org

The authors have asserted their rights under the Copyright, Designs and Patents Act, 1988, to be identified as the authors of this Work.

The opinions expressed in this book are those of the authors and do not necessarily reflect the official policy of the General Synod or The Archbishops' Council of the Church of England.

Scripture quotations from
The New Revised Standard Version of the Bible, copyright 1989 by the Division of Christian Education of the National Council of the Churches of the USA. Used by permission. All rights reserved.
The Revised English Bible © Oxford University Press and Cambridge University Press, 1961, 1970.

Material from *Common Worship: Services and Prayers for the Church of England* including the Psalter is copyright © The Archbishops' Council 2000 2008 and is used with permission.

Cover and contents design by David McNeill, Revo Design.

CONTENTS

Welcome to Pilgrim — 4

About the Authors and Contributors — 6

Introduction to The Eucharist — 7

The Eucharist

Session One: Your ancestors ate manna in the wilderness — 11

Session Two: This is my body broken for you — 21

Session Three: He was made known to them in the breaking of the bread — 29

Session Four: If you hear my voice and open the door, I will come in and eat with you — 39

Session Five: Do this to remember me — 47

Session Six: I am the bread of life — 55

Notes — 64

WELCOME TO *PILGRIM*

Welcome to this course of exploration into the truth of the Christian faith as it has been revealed in Jesus Christ and lived out in his Church down through the centuries.

The aim of this course is to help people explore what it means to be disciples of Jesus Christ. From the very beginning of his ministry, Jesus called people to follow him and become his disciples. The first disciples were called to be with Jesus and to be sent out (Mark 3.14). The Church in every generation shares in the task of helping others hear Christ's call to follow him and to live in his service.

The *Pilgrim* material consists of two groups of four short courses. The **Follow** stage is designed for those who are beginning to explore the faith and what following Jesus will mean. It focuses on four great texts which have been particularly significant to Christian people from the earliest days of the Church:

- The Baptismal Questions (drawn from the Creeds)
- The Lord's Prayer
- The Beatitudes
- The Commandments

'Follow' is a beginning in the Christian journey. There is much still to be learned. The four courses in the **Grow** stage – of which this is one – aim to take you further and deeper, building on the Follow stage. They focus on:

- The Creeds
- The Eucharist (and the whole life of prayer and worship)
- The Bible
- The Church and the kingdom (living your whole life as a disciple)

We hope that, in the Grow stage, people will learn the essentials for a life of discipleship. We hope that you will do this in the company of a small group of fellow travellers: people like you who want to find out more about the Christian faith and are considering its claims and challenges.

The material in the Grow stage can also be used helpfully by people who have been Christians for many years as a way of deepening their discipleship.

We have designed the material in the Grow stage so that it can be led by the members of the group: you don't need an expert or a teacher to guide you through. *Pilgrim* aims to help you learn by encouraging you to practise the ancient disciplines of biblical reflection and prayer which have always been at the heart of the living out of Christian faith.

The format is similar to the Follow stage. Each book has six sessions and, in each session, you will find:

- a **theme**
- some **opening prayers**
- a '**conversation-starter**'
- an opportunity to reflect on a **reading** from Scripture (the Bible)
- a short **reflection** on the theme from a contemporary Christian writer
- **some questions** to address together
- a '**journeying on**' section
- **some closing prayers**
- finally, there are selected quotations from the great tradition of Christian writing to aid further reflection.

You will find a greater emphasis in the Grow stage on learning to tell the story of God's work in your life to others as every disciple is called to be a witness. You will also find a greater emphasis on learning to live out your faith in everyday life. The Journeying On section includes an individual challenge for the week ahead and you are encouraged to share your progress as part of the Conversation as you meet for the next session.

An audio recording of the Reflection is available online. You will also find a short film for each session online at www.pilgrimcourse.org. The films in the Grow section are designed to help the group explore the theme in more depth and should normally be used after the Reflection and questions for discussion.

About the Authors and Contributors

Authors

Stephen Cottrell is the Bishop of Chelmsford
Steven Croft is the Bishop of Sheffield
Paula Gooder is a leading New Testament writer and lecturer
Robert Atwell is the Bishop of Exeter

Contributors

Simon Jones is the Chaplain of Merton College Oxford
Angela Tilby is a Canon of Christ Church Oxford and Continuing Ministerial Development Adviser for the Diocese of Oxford
John Inge is the Bishop of Worcester
John Pritchard is the Bishop of Oxford

INTRODUCTION TO *THE EUCHARIST*

Many years ago, I visited Mother Teresa's home for the destitute in Calcutta. As the sick and dying were brought in off the streets, they were laid on beds in cubicles where sisters washed their bodies and tended their sores. Above each bed was a sign in English fixed to the wall which said, 'The Body of Christ'. There is a link between our sharing in the Eucharist, our calling to be Christ's body in the world, and our service to others. As Jesus says in the parable of the sheep and goats, 'Just as you did it to the least of my brothers and sisters, you did it to me' (Matthew 25.40). To put it crudely, if we can't recognize the presence of Christ in the destitute and dying we are unlikely to recognize him in the breaking of the bread.

Historians tell us that the oldest religious ritual continuously observed in the world is Passover, when each year Jews commemorate their escape from slavery in Egypt. Like the Passover, the Eucharist is anchored in history and is celebrated by Christians the world over as a memorial of Christ's saving passion and resurrection. 'Do this in remembrance of me,' says Jesus, and for 2,000 years Christians have faithfully obeyed his command. It is why the Eucharist stands at the heart of Christian worship.

We do not know for certain whether or not the Last Supper Jesus held with his disciples on the night he was betrayed was a Passover meal, but it is likely. Throughout his ministry Jesus certainly had special fellowship meals with his disciples and he had the habit of breaking bread and sharing it. It was this characteristic action that opened the eyes of two disciples to his identity at Emmaus after his resurrection. At the Last Supper in the Upper Room, as Jesus broke the bread and blessed God for the wine, he associated these things with his own imminent death and thereby gave to them a spiritual significance that continues to shape the Christian community.

Christians celebrate this action in a variety of contexts and in a variety of ways. Like all meals it can be anything from a banquet, complete with exquisite music and ceremony, to a picnic where the emphasis is on simplicity and informality. The titles that Christians give to the service also vary. Some refer to it as the Lord's Supper, emphasizing the fact that at heart this is a sacred meal. Anglicans tend to call it either Holy Communion or the Eucharist.

The title Holy Communion reminds us that we are not observers but participants, guests at the Lord's Table who feeds us spiritually with his body and blood. The title Eucharist, meaning thanksgiving, is an ancient one as the Greek origin of the word implies. We give thanks for all that God has given us in Christ. This is summed up in the great Prayer of Thanksgiving or Eucharistic Prayer that the priest presiding at the service prays in the name of all assembled. The title Mass, commonly used by Roman Catholics, derives from the Latin of the closing words of the service, 'Go in peace to love and serve the Lord.' We gather around God's table to remember Christ's sacrifice before being sent out as a 'living sacrifice' to live and work to God's praise and glory. Whatever title is used, it is the same God who invites us to his table as a foretaste of the heavenly banquet he has prepared for all people.

There is nothing automatic about this sacramental meal, this 'outward and visible sign' of God's abundant grace. It is why Anglicans hesitate to define *how* God is present. As the poet John Donne famously wrote, 'He was the Word that spake it; he took the bread and brake it; and what that Word did make it, I do believe and take it.'[1] Augustine went as far as to suggest that it is the sacrament of ourselves that is placed on the Lord's Table and which we receive. 'Be then', he says, 'a member of Christ's body so that your Amen may accord with the truth.'[2] As we worship together we grow into becoming who we are meant to be: the Body of Christ.

Celebrating the hospitality of God, praising God for all that he has done for us in Christ, communing with our risen Lord and being renewed in our service of others are all aspects of the Eucharist that we will explore in this course, mindful of Paul's words that every time we break this bread and drink the cup we 'proclaim the Lord's death until he comes' (1 Corinthians 11.26).

Although the text for this part of *Pilgrim* is the service book for Holy Communion that is used in your local church, and we would encourage you to get hold of a copy and look at it alongside your participation in this course, there is one prayer that is particularly worth holding on to. It is the one that is often said after everyone has received communion. It offers thanks that God has fed us with the body and blood of Jesus; and we remember that the word Eucharist means 'thanksgiving'. It reminds us that we must offer our souls and bodies – our whole selves – as a living sacrifice to God (Romans 12.1–2). All worship, whatever the particular service, is about this offering of us. It says that we must be sent out to live and work to God's praise and glory. There is a rhythm to Christian worship: we are gathered in and we are sent out. Holy Communion is rations for the journey of life. It is also a foretaste of the banquet of heaven.

ROBERT ATWELL

**Almighty God,
we thank you for feeding us
with the body and blood of your son, Jesus Christ.
Through him we offer you our souls and bodies
to be a living sacrifice.
Send us out in the power of your Spirit
to live and work
to your praise and glory.
Amen.**

SESSION ONE:
YOUR ANCESTORS ATE MANNA IN THE WILDERNESS

pilgrim

In this session we are looking at worship as communion with God.

Opening Prayers

I am the bread of life,
anyone who comes to me shall not hunger,
anyone who believes in me shall never thirst.
Alleluia. Lord, give us this bread always.

The bread of God comes down from heaven,
and gives life to the world.
Alleluia. Lord, give us this bread always.

Anyone who eats my flesh and drinks my blood has eternal life
And I will raise him up on the last day.
Alleluia. Lord, give us this bread always.

It is the spirit that gives life; the flesh is of no avail.
The words I speak, they are spirit and they are life.
Alleluia. Lord, give us this bread always.

Walk with us, Lord,
Along the road of resurrection!
Explain for us, so slow to believe,
the things that scripture says of you.
Break the bread of the Eucharist with us
whenever we share our lives with our brothers and sisters.
Stay with us each time night approaches
and the daylight fades in our hearts.
Amen.

Conversation

If someone stopped you in the street and asked, why do you worship, what is it for, how would you reply? And what have been your best and most moving experiences of worship?

Reflecting on Scripture

Reading

Jesus said, 'I am the bread of life. [49]Your ancestors ate the manna in the wilderness, and they died. [50]This is the bread that comes down from heaven, so that one may eat of it and not die. [51]I am the living bread that came down from heaven. Whoever eats of this bread will live for ever; and the bread that I will give for the life of the world is my flesh.'
[52]The Jews then disputed among themselves, saying, 'How can this man give us his flesh to eat?' [53]So Jesus said to them, 'Very truly, I tell you, unless you eat the flesh of the Son of Man and drink his blood, you have no life in you. [54]Those who eat my flesh and drink my blood have eternal life, and I will raise them up on the last day; [55]for my flesh is true food and my blood is true drink. [56]Those who eat my flesh and drink my blood abide in me, and I in them. [57]Just as the living Father sent me, and I live because of the Father, so whoever eats me will live because of me. [58]This is the bread that came down from heaven, not like that which your ancestors ate, and they died. But the one who eats this bread will live for ever.'

JOHN 6.48–58

Explanatory note
In this passage Jesus is referring to the story in Exodus 16.1–36, in which God's people, having just escaped from slavery in Egypt, found themselves in the desert with no food. God miraculously fed them with quail and with a pale, flaky substance that they called manna (the word means literally 'what now?').

- Read the passage through once
- Keep a few moments' silence
- Read the passage a second time with different voices
- Invite everyone to say aloud a word or phrase that strikes them

- Read the passage a third time
- Share together what this word or phrase might mean and what questions it raises

Reflection
STEPHEN COTTRELL

When I was a stranger you welcomed me

One of the most basic, but often overlooked, symbols of the Christian faith is a table. Think of almost any church you have been into and you will find one. Sometimes it is very grand, high and lifted up and bedecked with candles; sometimes it is plain and unadorned. But it is there for a reason. It signifies one of the most fundamental truths of the Christian faith: that we are welcome; that in the words of Jesus on the night before he died, 'there is a place prepared for us' (see John 14.2). In Jesus, God has done everything that is needed for us to enjoy eternal life with him. That being welcomed into the life of God is symbolized by the table. As we shall see in a later session, it is also a foreshadowing of the banquet of heaven itself.

And Christian worship is very often gathered around the table in the service we call the Eucharist or Holy Communion or The Lord's Supper. Like the very first Christians we worship by coming together to break bread (Acts 20.7). It is the basic act of Christian worship, instituted by Jesus himself on the night before he died. It is also very human. Meeting to eat is a wonderful way to bring people together. But it's not just the food itself that creates hospitality – think of canteen meals! Good hosts offer friendship too; the eating and being together around the table create that hospitable place, where conversations can occur and relationships develop.

> *Good hosts offer friendship too.*

In the Eucharist God offers us such hospitality: God is the host, and we are the guests.

The service of Holy Communion has two distinct parts –

- **The Liturgy of the Word** (the readings from Scripture, the sermon, the Creed and the Intercessions).
- **The Liturgy of the Sacrament** (the Peace, the Preparation of the Table, the Great Prayer of Thanksgiving over the bread and wine, the Lord's Prayer, the breaking of the bread and the giving of Communion itself).

There are, as it were, two tables: the table where we gather to break open God's word; and the table where we gather to break open the bread. Around both these tables God gathers and feeds his people.

In the Church of England the Eucharist often begins with the words, 'The Lord is here!' God is taking the initiative. We gather around God's table and in God's presence. We don't need to invite God to join us. He is already here waiting to welcome us.

And, of course, God is everywhere – not just in church! God welcomes me wherever I am, so it is possible to worship anywhere and at any time. But the Sunday gathering of the Christian community is the place where this is made real. We Christians keep coming back to the table of the Lord because here we experience God's hospitality, and here we learn to be hospitable ourselves.

> **In short**
>
> In the Eucharist, God is the host and we are the guests. We gather around his table and learn from his hospitality how to be hospitable ourselves.

For discussion

- How has your life been enriched by hospitality? Share some experiences of welcoming others or being welcomed in yourself.
- What elements in the worship you have attended remind you of God's welcome?

I am with you always

Sometimes it is easy to sense God's presence in worship. There is a description of a time like this in Exodus 15. The Israelites had just escaped from the oppressive regime in Egypt, and had experienced high drama as Moses led them through the Red Sea. They 'saw the great work that the Lord did' and rejoiced at the signs of God's protection. Their enthusiastic song of praise and thanks was accompanied by tambourines and dancing. It was the very first 'happy clappy' service!

But life isn't always like that! When the Israelites arrived in the desert, they didn't feel like worshipping God there. They struggled with the ongoing realities of daily life in a new situation, and it is not surprising that they reacted as they did. Grumbles and complaints like theirs are classic symptoms of what is sometimes called 'culture shock' – the stresses that understandably occur when people have to adapt to new surroundings, bereft of a known way of life while simultaneously working out how to manage unfamiliar situations.

But God was already there in the desert – and welcomed them generously, just as they were. Manna was a completely unexpected gift, totally unplanned by them. All of them received God's generosity – not just a select few. As a whole community the Israelites were delivered from Egypt and fed in the desert, and this story became part of their 'salvation history'. In Psalm 78 we read how they retold this story together in worship to pass the memory down the generations. In John 6 Jesus too remembered this story and used it to talk about the gift that he brings to us.

> *Manna was a completely unexpected gift.*

Whether the service is a Eucharist or not, meeting in worship can be a time when we are reminded of God's continuing welcome to his people and of all that God has done to make that welcome possible. When we worship we retell the story of our faith. We remind ourselves of all the ways God has met with us. We bring to God our hopes and needs, our joys and fears. God is our gracious host. God doesn't just welcome everyone. He welcomes everything about us.

> **In short**
> All services – whether a Eucharist or not – are times when we are reminded that God welcomes us as his people just as we are.

For discussion

- How do you feel that God is with you when you worship?
- What are the other times in your life when you have been aware of God's provision and welcome? How have these times become part of your own story? And how is it changing you?

Journeying On

During this next week, think about how the welcome you receive from God in worship can be imitated in your daily life in the welcome and hospitality you offer to others – strangers as well as fellow pilgrims. We will share with each other any conclusions we have come to at the start of the next session. And if you haven't done so already, get hold of a Holy Communion service booklet from your local church or download it from the internet and read through the service; see its structure and enjoy the beautiful language of its prayers.

Concluding Prayers

**The cup of blessing that we bless,
is it not a sharing in the blood of Christ?
The bread that we break,
is it not a sharing in the body of Christ?
Because there is one bread,
we who are many are one body,
for we all partake of the one bread.**

1 CORINTHIANS 10.16–17

Merciful God
You have called us to your table
Generous God
You have fed us with the bread of life
Abundant God
**Draw us and all people to the service of your Son;
And send us out to bring your peace and goodness to the world.
Amen.**

Wisdom for the Journey

On Sundays we hold an assembly of all our members, whether they live in the city or in the outlying districts. The memoirs of the apostles or the writings of the prophets are read, as long as time permits. When the reader has finished, the president of the assembly speaks to us urging everyone to imitate the examples of virtue we have heard in the readings. Then we all stand up together and pray. When we have finished praying, bread and wine and water are brought forward. The president offers prayers and gives thanks as well as possible, and the people give their assent by saying: 'Amen.' Then follows the distribution of the food over which the prayer of thanksgiving has been recited; everyone present receives some, and the deacons take some to those who are absent. The wealthy, if they wish, may make a contribution – they, themselves, decide the amount. The collection is placed in the custody of the president, who uses it to help the orphans and widows and all who for any reason are in distress, whether because they are sick, in prison, or away from home.

JUSTIN (C.100–165)

Do you wish to honour the body of the saviour? Then do not despise it when it is naked. Do not honour it in church with silk vestments while outside you are leaving it numb with cold and naked. He who said, 'This is my body', and made it so by his word, is the same that said, 'You saw me hungry and gave me no food. As you did it not to one of the least of my brothers and sisters, you did it not to me.' Honour him by sharing your property with the poor. What God needs is not golden cups but golden hearts.

JOHN CHRYSOSTOM (C.347–407)

The reason for our loving God *is* God. He is the initiator of our love and its final goal. God is loveable in himself and gives himself to us as the object of our love. He desires that our love for him should bring us happiness, and not be arid and barren. His love for us opens up inside us the way to love, and is the reward of our own reaching out in love. How gently he leads us in love's way, how generously he returns the love we give, how sweet he is to those who wait for him!

BERNARD OF CLAIRVAUX (1090–1153)

I hunger and I thirst:
Jesu, my manna be;
Ye living waters, burst
Out of the rock for me.

Thou bruised and broken Bread,
My life-long wants supply;
As living souls are fed,
O feed me, or I die.

J. S. B. MONSELL (1811–75)

The fundamental business of life is worship. At the root of all your being, your intellectual studies, the games you play, whatever it is, the impulse to do them well is and ought to be understood as being an impulse towards God, the source of all that is excellent. All life ought to be worship; and we know quite well there is no chance it will be worship unless we have times when we have worship and nothing else.

WILLIAM TEMPLE (1881–1944)

SESSION TWO:
THIS IS MY BODY BROKEN FOR YOU

pilgrim

In this session we are looking at the Eucharist as the pattern of all Christian worship.

Opening Prayers

I am the bread of life,
anyone who comes to me shall not hunger,
anyone who believes in me shall never thirst.
Alleluia. Lord, give us this bread always.

The bread of God comes down from heaven,
and gives life to the world.
Alleluia. Lord, give us this bread always.

Anyone who eats my flesh and drinks my blood has eternal life
And I will raise him up on the last day.
Alleluia. Lord, give us this bread always.

It is the spirit that gives life; the flesh is of no avail.
the words I speak, they are spirit and they are life.
Alleluia. Lord, give us this bread always.

Walk with us, Lord,
Along the road of resurrection!
Explain for us, so slow to believe,
the things that scripture says of you.
Break the bread of the Eucharist with us
whenever we share our lives with our brothers and sisters.
Stay with us each time night approaches
and the daylight fades in our hearts.
Amen.

Conversation

Have you thought of any ways you can imitate God's hospitality in your daily life? Who are the strangers and fellow pilgrims that God might be asking you to show welcome to?

And as a way into this session, share with each other any memories you have of significant meals in your life. Why were they important? What made them special?

Reflecting on Scripture

Reading

For I received from the Lord what I also handed on to you, that the Lord Jesus on the night when he was betrayed took a loaf of bread, [24]and when he had given thanks, he broke it and said, 'This is my body that is for you. Do this in remembrance of me.' [25]In the same way he took the cup also, after supper, saying, 'This cup is the new covenant in my blood. Do this, as often as you drink it, in remembrance of me.' [26]For as often as you eat this bread and drink the cup, you proclaim the Lord's death until he comes. [27]Whoever, therefore, eats the bread or drinks the cup of the Lord in an unworthy manner will be answerable for the body and blood of the Lord. [28]Examine yourselves, and only then eat of the bread and drink of the cup

1 CORINTHIANS 11.23–28

Explanatory note

These words are often known as 'the words of institution' because they command Jesus' followers to keep on remembering Jesus by breaking bread and sharing wine. They occur in slightly different forms here in 1 Corinthians 11.23–28 and in three out of the four Gospels (Matthew 26.26–29; Mark 14.22–25 and Luke 22.19–21).

The words in 1 Corinthians are believed to have been the first ones written down (in approximately the mid-50s AD, about 20 years or so before the words in the Gospels reached their final form).

- Read the passage through once
- Keep a few moments' silence
- Read the passage a second time with different voices
- Invite everyone to say aloud a word or phrase that strikes them
- Read the passage a third time
- Share together what this word or phrase might mean and what questions it raises

Reflection

SIMON JONES

Remembering

In a society that values bodily perfection, the invitation to break bread to remember a broken man is deeply countercultural. But this is precisely what Christians do every time they celebrate the Eucharist together. At the Last Supper, the bread that Jesus takes is broken so that it can be shared among the disciples. This simple, everyday act of breaking bread is not just a practical necessity to enable a group of first-century Jews to share food among themselves. Much more significantly, it points forward to the death by which Christ brings salvation to the world, and provides the means by which his followers will remember that death for generations to come. 'Do this in remembrance of me' (1 Corinthians 11.24).

> The celebration of Holy Communion is an act of the Church. We declare and remember the saving acts of God. It is something we do together – we are the priestly people of God. It is something that requires the presidency of an ordained minister – because the ordained minister, acting as it were as the representative of Christ, brings the universal to the local. The priest ensures that the service we offer is not just our private celebration but the one sacrifice of praise of the one, holy, catholic and apostolic Church of Jesus Christ.

As we sift through our memories of past events and people we have known it is easy to be forgetful or to become confused about some of the details. But then, prompted by something or someone, we can be reminded of them again. The Eucharist is different. We were not present at the Last Supper, nor did we stand with Mary and John at the foot of the cross. We're therefore not remembering something that we witnessed for ourselves at first hand. Despite this obvious fact, Christians believe that, at the Eucharist, we remember Jesus and, as we do so, experience his presence among us. This remembering is much more profound than being reminded of a happy or sad event from our past, like a favourite holiday or the end of a relationship.

At the Eucharist, the memorial of Christ's death and resurrection is made possible through the transforming power of the Holy Spirit. The Spirit doesn't just remind us that Christ died and was raised on the third day, but enables us to be transformed again and again by the events of Good Friday and Easter. In this way we become more fully the people God calls us to be. Those who, through baptism, have died to sin and been raised to new life with Christ (see Romans 6.5–11) experience this transformation again and again as the Eucharist is celebrated together as members of the Church, which Paul describes as the body of Christ (see 1 Corinthians 12.27).

> **In short**
>
> When we remember Jesus in the Eucharist, we are transformed again and again by Jesus' death and resurrection and so become more fully the people that God wanted us to be.

For discussion

- As you have begun to grow in the Christian life, what does the Eucharist and receiving Holy Communion mean to you?
- What are you remembering?
- How important is it for you to remember the death and resurrection of Jesus when you worship at the Eucharist, or at any other service for that matter?

A sacrifice of praise

Like the apostles who were invited by Jesus to share a meal with him on the night before his death, whenever we respond to Jesus' invitation to 'do this in remembrance of me', he promises to be with us, and to feed us with his body and blood. He does this to bring us into communion with him and with our fellow Christians, strengthening us with his presence as we seek to live as his disciples. 'For as often as you eat this bread and drink the cup, you proclaim the Lord's death until he comes' (1 Corinthians 11.26).

> Jesus' death is a sacrifice motivated by love.

For Christians, Jesus' death on the cross is a sacrifice – a sacrifice motivated by love. As Jesus says in John's Gospel, 'No one has greater love than this, to lay down one's life for one's friends' (John 15.13).

But how do we know it is a sacrifice? Well, Jesus' actions, taking and breaking the bread and pouring out the wine, are like an acted parable. Although the disciples would not have understood it at the time, Jesus is giving them a way of interpreting his death correctly. Like the bread broken, Jesus' body is broken on the cross. Like the wine poured out, Jesus' blood is shed for us.

There can be no repetition of Jesus' sacrifice, but whenever we celebrate the Eucharist we are in communion with the risen Christ whose sacrifice has brought us peace with God. This is why the table around which we gather is also called an altar, a place where the sacrifice of Christ is recalled and its benefits made present.

To participate in the Eucharist is to recognize our brokenness, as individuals and as communities, and our need to be united with Christ in order to be made whole. As we have explored in other sessions in *Pilgrim*, Christians believe that Jesus was broken to save us from our sins and brokenness. We now offer the bread and cup to God as a sacrifice of praise and thanksgiving. Made whole through our communion with Christ's sacrificial death, we offer our lives to God as a living sacrifice. The words that we often pray together after Communion express this: 'we offer you our souls and bodies to be a living sacrifice'.

This is true of all worship; even the simplest song of a few Christians gathered in a school hall, or the grandest service you can possibly imagine is an offering of praise, the sacrifice of our hearts and the alignment of our lives to God. As we gather around Christ's table, the one whom we remember offers us a piece of his broken body to make us whole, and sends us out as members of his body to share his life in the brokenness of the world.

> **In short**
>
> When we participate in the Eucharist we recall Jesus' sacrifice for us, recognize our own brokenness, remember that he was broken to make us whole and offer him our souls and bodies as a sacrifice of thanksgiving for all he has done for us.

For discussion

- What does sacrificial living mean to you and your Christian community?
- How does worship, and especially the Eucharist, help you live the Christian life and offer your life as a sacrifice of praise?
- How does the double symbolism of table and altar help you think about the different ways we experience the Eucharist?

Journeying On

During this next week, think about how we are called to live out the sacrificial love we see in the death and resurrection of Jesus and which is made present for us in the Eucharist. What does it mean for us to live sacrificial lives? What sacrifices might God be asking you to make?

Concluding Prayers

**The cup of blessing that we bless,
is it not a sharing in the blood of Christ?
The bread that we break,
is it not a sharing in the body of Christ?
Because there is one bread,
we who are many are one body,
for we all partake of the one bread.**

1 CORINTHIANS 10.16–17

Merciful God
You have called us to your table
Generous God
You have fed us with the bread of life
Abundant God
Draw us and all people to the service of your Son;
And send us out to bring your peace and goodness to the world.
Amen.

Wisdom for the Journey

We do not consume the eucharistic bread and wine as if it were ordinary food and drink. We have been taught that just as Jesus Christ became a human being of flesh and blood by the power of the Word of God for our salvation, so also the food that our flesh and blood assimilate for their nourishment becomes the flesh and blood of this Jesus who became flesh by the power of his word in the prayer of thanksgiving.

JUSTIN (C.100-165)

I came to see that there is no space without God: space does not exist apart from God. God is in heaven, in hell, and beyond the seas. God lives in everything and enfolds everything. God embraces all that is, and is embraced by the universe: confined to no part within it, he encompasses all that exists. My soul drew joy from contemplating the mystery of God's wisdom, his sheer majesty, and I worshipped the eternity and immeasurable greatness of my Father and creator.

HILARY OF POITIERS (315-67)

Believers know the body of Christ if they do not neglect to be the body of Christ.

AUGUSTINE (354-430)

Love is that liquor sweet and most divine,
Which my God feels as blood; but I, as wine.

GEORGE HERBERT (1593-1633)

SESSION THREE:
HE WAS MADE KNOWN TO THEM IN THE BREAKING OF THE BREAD

pilgrim

In this session we are looking at the intimacy we have with God in Holy Communion and how we are transformed by the encounter.

Opening Prayers

I am the bread of life,
anyone who comes to me shall not hunger,
anyone who believes in me shall never thirst.
Alleluia. Lord, give us this bread always.

The bread of God comes down from heaven,
and gives life to the world.
Alleluia. Lord, give us this bread always.

Anyone who eats my flesh and drinks my blood has eternal life
And I will raise him up on the last day.
Alleluia. Lord, give us this bread always.

It is the spirit that gives life; the flesh is of no avail.
the words I speak, they are spirit and they are life.
Alleluia. Lord, give us this bread always.

Walk with us, Lord,
Along the road of resurrection!
Explain for us, so slow to believe,
the things that scripture says of you.
Break the bread of the Eucharist with us
whenever we share our lives with our brothers and sisters.
Stay with us each time night approaches
and the daylight fades in our hearts.
Amen.

Conversation

Share with each other your thoughts about how God might be asking us to live sacrificially. Then in preparation for this session share any experiences of an encounter that transformed you. It will probably be with another person. What happened? What was it about this person that was so transformative?

Reflecting on Scripture

Reading

Now on that same day two of them were going to a village called Emmaus, about seven miles from Jerusalem, [14]and talking with each other about all these things that had happened. [15]While they were talking and discussing, Jesus himself came near and went with them, [16]but their eyes were kept from recognizing him. [17]And he said to them, 'What are you discussing with each other while you walk along?' They stood still, looking sad. [18]Then one of them, whose name was Cleopas, answered him, 'Are you the only stranger in Jerusalem who does not know the things that have taken place there in these days?' [19]He asked them, 'What things?' They replied, 'The things about Jesus of Nazareth, who was a prophet mighty in deed and word before God and all the people, [20]and how our chief priests and leaders handed him over to be condemned to death and crucified him. [21]But we had hoped that he was the one to redeem Israel. Yes, and besides all this, it is now the third day since these things took place. [22]Moreover, some women of our group astounded us. They were at the tomb early this morning, [23]and when they did not find his body there, they came back and told us that they had indeed seen a vision of angels who said that he was alive. [24]Some of those who were with us went to the tomb and found it just as the women had said; but they did not see him.' [25]Then he said to them, 'Oh, how foolish you are, and how slow of heart to believe all that the prophets have declared! [26]Was it not necessary that the Messiah should suffer these things and then enter into his glory?' [27]Then beginning with Moses and all the prophets, he interpreted to them the things about himself in all the scriptures.

[28]As they came near the village to which they were going, he walked ahead as if he were going on. [29]But they urged him strongly, saying, 'Stay with us, because it is almost evening and the day is now nearly over.' So he went in to stay with them. [30]When he was at the table with them, he took bread, blessed

and broke it, and gave it to them. ³¹Then their eyes were opened, and they recognized him; and he vanished from their sight. ³²They said to each other, 'Were not our hearts burning within us while he was talking to us on the road, while he was opening the scriptures to us?' ³³That same hour they got up and returned to Jerusalem; and they found the eleven and their companions gathered together. ³⁴They were saying, 'The Lord has risen indeed, and he has appeared to Simon!' ³⁵Then they told what had happened on the road, and how he had been made known to them in the breaking of the bread.

LUKE 24.13–35

- Read the passage through once – though as this is a longer passage than usual you may decide to omit the first reading
- Keep a few moments' silence
- Read the passage a second time with different voices
- Invite everyone to say aloud a word or phrase that strikes them
- Read the passage a third time
- Share together what this word or phrase might mean and what questions it raises

Reflection   ANGELA TILBY

The Eucharist transforms our lives

All Christian worship is, potentially, an encounter with the risen Lord. When we meet him in worship, God calls us into a future that is already his and we offer ourselves to be transformed. The Eucharist, perhaps more than any other form of Christian worship, makes this transformation vivid and real. This is because it brings us directly into Christ's presence, not only through Scripture, but by a special kind of remembering that makes his Easter victory present to us. The bread and wine, ordinary food and drink, become charged with the memory of Christ's death and resurrection. For some Christians this is focused in the bread and wine itself. The consecrated bread and wine are lifted up so that people can see that 'The Lord is here'. For others the bread and wine act as reminders that point to the Lord's spiritual presence with his people. This presence of Jesus in Holy Communion is called a sacrament. A sacrament, as we shall explore in a later session, is an 'outward and visible sign of an inward and spiritual grace'. How this happens has been disputed by Christians over the centuries and has, sadly, led to some divisions between different branches of the Christian Church.

This explains the various ways the Eucharist is celebrated, and the different importance that different Christians give to it and even the fact that we have more than one name for the service. But all Christians of whatever tradition are united around this truth: the Lord who died on the cross for us opens his arms and longs to feeds us with his risen life. Jesus is the one 'in whom all our hungers are satisfied'. It is this story of his transforming love that we celebrate in Holy Communion and in all our worship.

> In the Church of England you need to be baptized before you can receive Holy Communion. Many churches admit children to Communion before Confirmation, but it would still be regarded as desirable and necessary that young people and adults make their own commitment of faith in Confirmation before beginning that lifelong journey of discipleship that is fed by Word and Sacrament around the table of the Lord. And because it is Jesus we meet and receive in Holy Communion, we need to prepare ourselves. The prayers of penitence at the beginning of the service are very important. But we should also pray before we come to Church, asking that God himself will make our hearts ready to receive him. As one of the prayers immediately before receiving Holy Communion puts it: 'Lord I am not worthy to receive you, but only say the word, and I shall be healed.'

The story of the Emmaus road underscores this theme. The disciples of Jesus are living with unmet hopes and deep grief. They meet a stranger on the road who walks alongside them. In his company they find they are able to tell their story and to express their sorrows and regret. Jesus listens to all that they have to say and then responds to them, opening the Scriptures and helping them to see that his death has not been the end of everything, but the moment of true liberation and transformation. Then, at the meal that they share together, he breaks bread – and they see him as he really is. The risen Christ meets them in the breaking of the bread. They cannot sustain the vision – Christ vanishes from their sight. But they are changed: 'Were not our hearts burning within us while he was talking to us on the road, while he was opening the scriptures to us?' Their hunger for hope, meaning and restoration is satisfied.

> **In short**
> Christians have many different views of the Eucharist but we are all united in believing that the Jesus who died on the cross for us is the one in whom all our hungers are satisfied.

For discussion

- When you worship, how are you aware of Christ's risen presence?
- And what sort of worship makes your heart burn within you?

Eucharistic living

As with all Christian worship – be it the simplest service of the Word, a pentecostal extravaganza or Holy Communion itself – we come as the selves that we are, with our particular strengths and weaknesses, virtues and frailties. We bring with us the whole network of relationships in which we live and work and struggle and dream. All this is raw material for transformation and is symbolized by the bread and wine, the work of human hands.

We come as the selves that we are.

But we are not present merely as individuals. Like the disciples on the Emmaus road, we come in company with one another, with shared memories and doubts and hopes. Together we praise God, and confess our need of God's goodness and grace in our lives. The risen Christ draws near to us as he did on the Emmaus road and we hear his promise to us in the Gospel. Then we see and hear how Jesus took the bread, blessed it, broke it and gave it to his disciples. The ordinary fabric of our lives is taken up into Christ's risen life and given back to us, charged with the hope and joy that comes from God's future. The Eucharist transforms us into kingdom people who are called to share our bread with the hungry and bring life and hope to the world.

In the Eucharist we are always being made new. This is beautifully expressed in the special prayer, the 'Collect' for the Second Sunday after the feast of the Epiphany:

Almighty God,
in Christ you make all things new,
transform the poverty of our nature
by the riches of your grace
and in the renewal of our lives
make known your heavenly glory
through Jesus Christ our Lord. Amen.

> **In short**
>
> In the Eucharist, we do not come just as individuals but with all our networks of relationships. There the whole of our lives are caught up into the life of the risen Christ and given back to us renewed.

For discussion

- How do you think you should prepare for worship? And how would you advise others?
- Jesus took bread, blessed it, broke it and gave it. How might this be a pattern for Christian living?

Journeying On

During this next week, think how worship forms your life and shapes who you are. How might God be taking, blessing, breaking and using you in his service? Ponder each word carefully. Take. Bless. Break. Share. How is this happening in your life? How is God transforming you; and how does God want to increase it within you, so that your life mirrors the offering of Christ?

Concluding Prayers

**The cup of blessing that we bless,
is it not a sharing in the blood of Christ?
The bread that we break,
is it not a sharing in the body of Christ?
Because there is one bread,
we who are many are one body,
for we all partake of the one bread.**

1 CORINTHIANS 10.16–17

Merciful God
You have called us to your table
Generous God
You have fed us with the bread of life
Abundant God
**Draw us and all people to the service of your Son;
And send us out to bring your peace and goodness to the world.
Amen.**

Wisdom for the Journey

In the same way that earthly bread, having received the invocation of God, is no longer ordinary bread but Eucharist, made up of two components, one earthly and the other heavenly, so our bodies that share in the Eucharist are no longer corruptible because they have the hope of resurrection.

IRENAEUS (130–C.200)

Calling her children around her the Church nourishes them with holy milk, that is with the infant Word … the Word is everything to a child; both Father and Mother, both instructor and nurse. 'Eat my flesh', he says, and 'Drink my blood.' The Lord supplies us with these intimate nutrients. He delivers over his flesh and pours out his blood and nothing is lacking for the growth of his children. O incredible mystery!

CLEMENT OF ALEXANDRIA (150–215)

When you approach the altar, do not present your hands spread out or your fingers separated, but instead make a throne with your left hand for your right hand since it is to receive the King, and receiving the body of Christ in the hollow of your hand, say 'Amen'.

CYRIL OF JERUSALEM (C.315–386)

At Emmaus the two disciples set the table, serve the food, and in the breaking of bread discover the God whom they failed to come to know in the explanation of the scriptures. It was not in hearing the precepts of God that they were enlightened, but when they carried them out.

GREGORY THE GREAT (540–604)

Soul of Christ, sanctify me,
body of Christ, save me,
blood of Christ, inebriate me,
water from the side of Christ, wash me.
Passion of Jesus, strengthen me.
O good Jesus, hear me:
hide me within your wounds
and let me never be separated from you.
From the wicked enemy defend me,
in the hour of my death, call me
and bid me come to you,
so that with your saints I may praise you
for ever and ever. Amen.

ANONYMOUS (FOURTEENTH CENTURY)

The country parson being to administer the sacraments, is at a stand with himself, how or what behaviour to assume for so holy things. Especially at communion times he is in a great confusion, as being not only to receive God, but to break and administer him. Neither finds he any issue in this, but to throw himself down at the throne of grace, saying 'Lord, thou knowest what thou didst when thou appointedst it to be done thus; therefore do thou fulfill what thou didst appoint; for thou art not only the feast, but the way to it.'

GEORGE HERBERT (1593–1633)

Here our humblest homage pay we;
Here in loving reverence bow;
Here for faith's discernment pray we,
Lest we fail to know thee now.
Alleluya,
Thou art here, we ask not how.

G. H. BOURNE (1840–1925)

SESSION FOUR:
IF YOU HEAR MY VOICE AND OPEN THE DOOR, I WILL COME IN AND EAT WITH YOU

pilgrim

In this session we are looking at worship as a sign and foretaste of heaven.

Opening Prayers

I am the bread of life,
anyone who comes to me shall not hunger,
anyone who believes in me shall never thirst.
Alleluia. Lord, give us this bread always.

The bread of God comes down from heaven,
and gives life to the world.
Alleluia. Lord, give us this bread always.

Anyone who eats my flesh and drinks my blood has eternal life
And I will raise him up on the last day.
Alleluia. Lord, give us this bread always.

It is the spirit that gives life; the flesh is of no avail.
the words I speak, they are spirit and they are life.
Alleluia. Lord, give us this bread always.

Walk with us, Lord,
Along the road of resurrection!
Explain for us, so slow to believe,
the things that scripture says of you.
Break the bread of the Eucharist with us
whenever we share our lives with our brothers and sisters.
Stay with us each time night approaches
and the daylight fades in our hearts.
Amen.

Conversation

How do you think worship shapes your life? Have you been able to think of ways God is blessing, breaking and using you?

Then for this session turn your minds to thoughts of heaven. When you think of heaven, what images come to mind? Share them with each other.

Reflecting on Scripture

Reading

'I know your works; you are neither cold nor hot. I wish that you were either cold or hot. ¹⁶So, because you are lukewarm, and neither cold nor hot, I am about to spit you out of my mouth. ¹⁷For you say, "I am rich, I have prospered, and I need nothing." You do not realize that you are wretched, pitiable, poor, blind, and naked. ¹⁸Therefore I counsel you to buy from me gold refined by fire so that you may be rich; and white robes to clothe you and to keep the shame of your nakedness from being seen; and salve to anoint your eyes so that you may see. ¹⁹I reprove and discipline those whom I love. Be earnest, therefore, and repent. ²⁰Listen! I am standing at the door, knocking; if you hear my voice and open the door, I will come in to you and eat with you, and you with me. ²¹To the one who conquers I will give a place with me on my throne, just as I myself conquered and sat down with my Father on his throne. ²²Let anyone who has an ear listen to what the Spirit is saying to the churches.'

REVELATION 3.15–22

Explanatory note
The start of the book of Revelation takes the form of letters to seven different churches in Asia Minor (what we would now call Turkey). One of these letters was to the church in Laodicea, well known for its water supply, which was lukewarm.

- Read the passage through once
- Keep a few moments' silence
- Read the passage a second time with different voices
- Invite everyone to say aloud a word or phrase that strikes them
- Read the passage a third time
- Share together what this word or phrase might mean and what questions it raises

Reflection

JOHN INGE

A sign and foretaste of the banquet of heaven

What will heaven be like? Christians have generally seemed to spend more time arguing about who will be admitted to heaven than thinking about its character. What, though, do we know about the nature of heaven? A moment's reflection reminds us that we have been told by Jesus himself that heaven is the place where God reigns, the place of God's kingdom. When we pray as he taught, we ask that 'God's kingdom will come on earth as it is in heaven.' And what is God's kingdom like? The Scriptures give us all sorts of images of the kingdom, many of which involve a feast. One of the recurring pictures of heaven and of humanity redeemed is that of a feast. 'On this mountain the Lord of hosts will make a feast of rich food, a feast of well-aged wines', proclaims the prophet Isaiah (Isaiah 25.6). As Jesus puts it, 'I tell you, many will come from east and west and will eat with Abraham and Isaac and Jacob in the kingdom of heaven' (Matthew 8.11).

> *Feasting is how we celebrate great occasions.*

That the kingdom of heaven should have been pictured as a feast in biblical times when food was often scarce is hardly surprising. Even today, though, when many of us in the affluent West have much more food than we need, the image of the feast is still a powerful one. Feasting is how we celebrate great occasions – as is evidenced by the way food dominates television adverts before Christmas. In a feast, what is at least as important as the food and drink, though, is the people with whom we share it. Eating and drinking on your own is no feast. Jesus proclaims to his disciples that he will drink the cup *with them* in the kingdom. Perhaps the best image we have of heaven, then, is of eating and drinking at a feast with Jesus and all the redeemed in his kingdom.

Therefore since the earliest times, Christians have believed that at the Eucharist we receive a foretaste of this kingdom feast. For it was at the Last Supper when Jesus was giving us the Eucharist that he talked to his disciples about drinking the cup with them in the kingdom (Matthew 26.29).

In the Church of England it is expected that Christians receive Holy Communion at least twice a year – at Christmas and Easter. But, of course, many churches celebrate Holy Communion every Sunday, and quite a number will have a Eucharist every day. You should not really receive Holy Communion more than once each day.

The usual method for receiving Holy Communion is to place one open hand upon another, so that the consecrated bread can be safely and easily placed in the centre of the palm; though there are some Christians who prefer to receive Communion directly onto their tongue.

But however we receive Holy Communion, Jesus is present with us. The Church has understood this in different ways down through the centuries. Sometimes this has led to painful disputes. At one end of the spectrum Christians have believed that the bread and wine become the body and blood of Jesus. At the other, what we are doing is a memorial meal in which Jesus is present in the gathered community that remember him. Between these is the view sometimes referred to as the 'real presence'. This declares that while the bread remains bread and the wine remains wine, they take on a new value and meaning that is the presence of Jesus himself.

Others have spoken about the Eucharist in this way all down the centuries of Christian history. The Holy Communion we share in church is not the fullness of the feast itself but a taste – a glimpse and effective sign of wonders to come and glory to be revealed. We live in a time poised between 'already' and 'not yet' in which we eat and drink with the risen Christ and receive his presence 'until he comes again' (1 Corinthians 11.26). We receive the bread of the world to come (John 6.48) and the new wine of the kingdom (Luke 5.37).

> **In short**
> One of the descriptions in the Bible of the glorious future God promises for his people is that of a great feast – in the Eucharist we get a glimpse of the feast that God promises to us all.

For discussion

- What do you think the heavenly feast will be like?
- How does our worship on earth prepare us?

The bread of tomorrow

Have you ever wondered why, in the Lord's Prayer, Jesus said 'Give us today our daily bread' rather than 'Give us today our bread' or 'Give us our daily bread'? The two words translated as 'day' and 'daily' are different in the Greek and the sentence might better be rendered 'Give us today our tomorrow's bread.' What does that mean? It could be 'the bread that has the character of the future feast'. That's what Early Church Fathers such as Cyprian and Jerome suggested when they translated it as 'Give us this day our supernatural or supersubstantial bread.' In other words, we are asking that we should be given the bread that we shall receive at the Heavenly Feast. In the Lord's Prayer, then, we pray for the things that make up the kingdom: the hallowing of God's name, the coming of his reign, the forgiveness of sins and the food of heaven.

> *It is the totality of our humanity that is redeemed.*

The Eucharist is a foretaste of the kingdom, a wonderful one that involves all of our humanity – body, mind and spirit. This reminds us that it is the totality of our humanity that is redeemed. Christ comes to us not just in the head, rationally; not just through our heart emotionally, but physically: 'God in the gut' as Graham Greene put it. By this heavenly food we are given the strength not only to pray but to labour for the kingdom of God of which we receive a foretaste.

In short

In the Lord's Prayer we ask that God will give us our 'daily bread'. This might mean that we are asking God to give us tomorrow's bread today – in other words, to give us a taste of our heavenly food.

For discussion

- Have you ever felt that in worship the life of tomorrow is breaking in to today? What was it like? What difference does it make?
- What is it about the Eucharist that feels like a feast to you?

Journeying On

Start thinking about your own pattern of worship. Do you attend each week? Do you need to establish a rule about this? What about the major festivals of the Christian year? Would it be a good idea to decide that these are times when you also should be gathered with God's people around the Lord's Table?

Concluding Prayers

The cup of blessing that we bless,
is it not a sharing in the blood of Christ?
The bread that we break,
is it not a sharing in the body of Christ?
Because there is one bread,
we who are many are one body,
for we all partake of the one bread.

1 CORINTHIANS 10.16–17

Merciful God
You have called us to your table
Generous God
You have fed us with the bread of life
Abundant God
Draw us and all people to the service of your Son;
And send us out to bring your peace and goodness to the world.
Amen.

Wisdom for the Journey

As this broken bread once scattered over the mountains has been gathered together to make a single loaf, so Lord gather your church together from the ends of the earth into your kingdom.

ANONYMOUS (LATE FIRST CENTURY)

Just as Scripture describes the unity of the faithful in the words: 'They were of one mind and heart in God,' so the image of the wine functions in the same way as that of the kneading of many grains into one visible loaf. Think how wine is made. Many grapes hang on the vine in clusters, but their juice flows together into an indivisible liquid once they are crushed. It was in these images that Christ our Lord signified to us that we should belong to him, when he hallowed the sacrament of our peace and unity on his table.

AUGUSTINE (354–430)

Christ gave us the Eucharist that we might by it attain unto endless day and the very table of Christ, and there [in heaven] receive in fullness and unto all satisfaction that of which we have been given the taste.

PETER CHRYSOLOGUS, FIFTH CENTURY

Let us receive Christ at our table now so as to be welcomed at his eternal banquet. Let us show hospitality to Christ present in the stranger now so that at the judgement he will not ignore us as strangers, but will welcome us as brothers and sisters into his kingdom.

GREGORY THE GREAT (540–604)

SESSION FIVE:
DO THIS TO REMEMBER ME

pilgrim

In this session we are looking at how worship shapes the whole of life.

Opening Prayers

I am the bread of life,
anyone who comes to me shall not hunger,
anyone who believes in me shall never thirst.
Alleluia. Lord, give us this bread always.

The bread of God comes down from heaven,
and gives life to the world.
Alleluia. Lord, give us this bread always.

Anyone who eats my flesh and drinks my blood has eternal life
And I will raise him up on the last day.
Alleluia. Lord, give us this bread always.

It is the spirit that gives life; the flesh is of no avail.
The words I speak, they are spirit and they are life.
Alleluia. Lord, give us this bread always.

Walk with us, Lord,
Along the road of resurrection!
Explain for us, so slow to believe,
the things that scripture says of you.
Break the bread of the Eucharist with us
whenever we share our lives with our brothers and sisters.
Stay with us each time night approaches
and the daylight fades in our hearts.
Amen.

Conversation

What do you think is a reasonable and realistic pattern for daily prayer and worship? What should all Christians aspire to; and what will your pattern be?

Then in preparation for this session think about the things we actually worship. If worship means literally, 'the things we give worth to', what are the things that actually take first place in your life?

Reflecting on Scripture

Reading

He said to them, 'I have eagerly desired to eat this Passover with you before I suffer; [16]for I tell you, I will not eat it until it is fulfilled in the kingdom of God.' [17]Then he took a cup, and after giving thanks he said, 'Take this and divide it among yourselves; [18]for I tell you that from now on I will not drink of the fruit of the vine until the kingdom of God comes.' [19]Then he took a loaf of bread, and when he had given thanks, he broke it and gave it to them, saying, 'This is my body, which is given for you. Do this in remembrance of me.' [20]And he did the same with the cup after supper, saying, 'This cup that is poured out for you is the new covenant in my blood.'

LUKE 22.15–20

Explanatory note

This is the version of the words of institution from Luke's Gospel (compare them with the ones from 1 Corinthians 11 that we saw in Session 2).

Notice that Luke's words have Jesus sharing two cups: one before the breaking of the bread and one after it. These two cups may be connected to two out of the four cups associated with the Jewish Passover meal.

- Read the passage through once
- Keep a few moments' silence
- Read the passage a second time with different voices
- Invite everyone to say aloud a word or phrase that strikes them
- Read the passage a third time
- Share together what this word or phrase might mean and what questions it raises

Reflection
STEPHEN COTTRELL

Community with God

Against all the beguiling philosophies of the world, the Christian faith makes this great claim: I worship, therefore I am.

At the heart of the Christian faith is the belief that we are made for community in God. 'The human heart is restless', wrote Augustine, 'until it finds its rest in God.' When we worship we become the people who find their rest and fulfilment in God. We become who we are meant to be. We enter into community with the God who, in Jesus, is revealed as a community of persons, Father, Son and Holy Spirit. This is the community that we are part of through our baptism. The Church is the community of persons who have been gathered together by Christ and have access to God. And worship is what we do.

Of course, it doesn't always feel like this when we worship. Sometimes we are distracted. Sometimes it is boring. Sometimes we don't know the hymns or are put off by the sermon. But it is still true. When we worship we enter deeply into that relationship with God that Jesus has made possible by his death and resurrection.

> In the Church of England there are many, many different types and styles of worship. But they are all doing the same thing: offering a sacrifice of thanks and praise to God. They are Services of the Word, where we gather around the table of the Word, search the Scriptures, confess our sins and sing God's praises. These services do not need to be led by an ordained minister. Sometimes they will be led by a Reader or Licensed Lay Minister, sometimes by a lay person authorized by the bishop. As the variety and reach of our worship develops, especially in what are called Fresh Expressions of church, more and more of our worship will be lay led. But the presiding minister of the Eucharist will always be a priest, and it is the job of the clergy and church council of a parish to have oversight of all the worship to ensure that what is celebrated and taught is the faith of Jesus Christ.

The Eucharist is the primary act of worship in the Church, the one service given us by Jesus himself. But as we have seen, it is also the pattern for all worship. Every time Christian people gather for worship and break open God's word and enjoy fellowship together and confess their need of God, then we are entering into the life of heaven. We are joining our voices with those of the saints and the angels who forever sing God's praises. We participate in the life to come. The life of tomorrow breaks into the life of today.

> **In short**
> When we worship we enter deeply into that relationship with God that Jesus made possible by his death and resurrection and are joining our voices with the saints and the angels who worship God continually.

For discussion

- What worship works best for you?
- Carry on thinking about your own pattern for worship and daily prayer. Discuss this with others, and begin to make some conclusions for your own life as a disciple of Christ.

Becoming what you worship

Worship changes us. This is why the Bible is so forceful in its condemnation of idolatry. If you worship something that isn't God – money or power for instance – then there is a very real danger that you will become like the thing you worship. But if we worship God ... If we sing God's praises ... If we look long and lovingly at Jesus ... If we receive his words of forgiveness, his bread of life, then we become like him. 'All of us, with unveiled faces, seeing the glory of the Lord ... are being transformed into the same image', says Paul (2 Corinthians 3.18).

It is for all these reasons that we must take worship very seriously. It's not that God needs our praises; rather we need to be made people who are thankful and adoring. (We are far too easily in love with ourselves!)

And because we are made for heaven, we are made for worship. It should be our joyful duty to be part of the worshipping community of our local church every Sunday. We should also try to observe the major festivals of the church year, especially Christmas, with the feast of the Incarnation; and Holy Week and Easter, when we recall Christ's passion, death and resurrection. And even if our church is not one that has the Eucharist as its main act of worship every Sunday, we should make sure that we receive Holy Communion as regularly as we can, and always at Christmas and Easter. As we have explored, the sacraments are channels of grace and living encounters with the risen Christ

Finally, Scripture also has some stern warnings about worship. 'I despise your festivals,' says God, 'Take away from me the noise of your songs; I will not listen to the melody of your harps. But let justice roll down like waters, and righteousness like an ever-flowing stream' (Amos 5.21, 23–24). For unless worship is changing us, so that our concerns and priorities are shaped by the concerns and priorities of God, and unless we are seeking God's justice and righteousness for the world, then our worship is worthless.

> **In short**
> We worship God not because he needs it or because it changes him, but because it changes us.

For discussion

- How might God be scandalized or despairing of his Church today and its worship?
- How does worship at our church shape our priorities and concerns in the world?

Journeying On

During this next week, think about how worship is changing the priorities and concerns of your life and what your response should be. How would you tell someone this story of what God has done in Christ and how is this experienced and lived out in worship? Be ready to share this with others in the group next time.

Concluding Prayers

**The cup of blessing that we bless,
is it not a sharing in the blood of Christ?
The bread that we break,
is it not a sharing in the body of Christ?
Because there is one bread,
we who are many are one body,
for we all partake of the one bread.**

1 CORINTHIANS 10.16–17

Merciful God
You have called us to your table
Generous God
You have fed us with the bread of life
Abundant God
**Draw us and all people to the service of your Son;
And send us out to bring your peace and goodness to the world.
Amen.**

Wisdom for the Journey

> Hasten to the springs, draw from the wells. In God alone is the wellspring of life, a spring whose waters will never fail you. In his light is to be found a light that nothing can darken. So desire that light which your eyes know not! Your inward eye is preparing to see the light. Your inward thirst burns to be quenched at the spring.

AUGUSTINE (354–430)

It is possible to regard worship as one of the greatest of humanity's mistakes; a form taken by the fantasy-life, the desperate effort of bewildered creatures to come to terms with the surrounding mystery. Or it may be accepted as the most profound of man's responses to reality; and more than this, the organ of his divine knowledge and the earnest of eternal life.

EVELYN UNDERHILL (1875-1941)

Was ever another command so obeyed? For century after century, spreading slowly to every continent and country and among every race on earth, this action has been done, in every conceivable human circumstance, for every conceivable human need from infancy and before it to extreme old age and after it, from the pinnacles of earthly greatness to the refuge of fugitives in the caves and dens of the earth. Men have found no better thing than this to do for kings at their crowning and for criminals going to the scaffold; for armies in triumph or for a bride and bridegroom in a little country church; for the proclamation of a dogma or for a good crop of wheat; for the wisdom of the parliament of a mighty nation or for a sick old woman afraid to die; for a schoolboy sitting an examination or for Columbus setting out to discover America; for the famine of whole provinces or for the soul of a dead lover. One could fill many pages with the reasons why men have done this, and not tell a hundredth part of them. And best of all, week by week and month by month, on a hundred thousand successive Sundays, faithfully, unfailingly, across all the parishes of Christendom, the pastors have done this just to *make* the *plebs sancta Dei* – the holy common people of God.

GREGORY DIX (1901-52)

The Risen Jesus who is the heart of the heavenly worship is also the Jesus who was crucified, and we share in heaven's worship only as sharing also in the Jesus who suffers in the world around us, reminding us to meet him there and to serve him in those who suffer.

MICHAEL RAMSEY (1904-88)

SESSION SIX:
I AM THE BREAD OF LIFE

pilgrim

In this session we are looking at the notion that the whole of life is sacramental.

Opening Prayers

I am the bread of life,
anyone who comes to me shall not hunger,
anyone who believes in me shall never thirst.
Alleluia. Lord, give us this bread always.

The bread of God comes down from heaven,
and gives life to the world.
Alleluia. Lord, give us this bread always.

Anyone who eats my flesh and drinks my blood has eternal life
And I will raise him up on the last day.
Alleluia. Lord, give us this bread always.

It is the spirit that gives life; the flesh is of no avail.
the words I speak, they are spirit and they are life.
Alleluia. Lord, give us this bread always.

Walk with us, Lord,
Along the road of resurrection!
Explain for us, so slow to believe,
the things that scripture says of you.
Break the bread of the Eucharist with us
whenever we share our lives with our brothers and sisters.
Stay with us each time night approaches
and the daylight fades in our hearts.
Amen.

Conversation

Share with each other as a way of summing up all that we have explored in this course the things that God has done for you in Christ that you particularly experience in worship. You might also like to mention where you have seen and encountered God in daily life, and what you think your future pattern of worship and daily prayer will be. Allow this session more time than usual and give each person in the group a chance to speak.

Reflecting on Scripture

Reading

Jesus said to them, 'I am the bread of life. Whoever comes to me will never be hungry, and whoever believes in me will never be thirsty. [36]But I said to you that you have seen me and yet do not believe. [37]Everything that the Father gives me will come to me, and anyone who comes to me I will never drive away; [38]for I have come down from heaven, not to do my own will, but the will of him who sent me. [39]And this is the will of him who sent me, that I should lose nothing of all that he has given me, but raise it up on the last day.'

JOHN 6.35–39

- Read the passage through once
- Keep a few moments' silence
- Read the passage a second time with different voices
- Invite everyone to say aloud a word or phrase that strikes them
- Read the passage a third time
- Share together what this word or phrase might mean and what questions it raises

Reflection   JOHN PRITCHARD

The sacramental principle

God uses material things as signs and pledges of his grace, and as a means by which we receive them. More than anywhere else we see this principle lived out in the life of Jesus himself. Jesus is the outward and visible sign of God's presence in the world always and everywhere. He was the human face of God, God's self-portrait. Quite simply, like Father, like Son.

Jesus seems to be claiming such a special sacramental identity when he says in John's Gospel, 'I am the bread of life. Whoever comes to me will never be hungry, and whoever believes in me will never be thirsty.' Christians recognize the truth of this sacramental identity as they understand themselves to be receiving the life of Christ in the bread and wine of the Eucharist.

Once we've recognized what we call the 'sacramental principle' in the person of Jesus it becomes easier to see it working out all over the place. The God who we recognize in Jesus is disclosed in and through people, actions and things that carry what we might call 'added weight'. For example, things such as water, fire, bread, wine and oil may all carry added weight in particular situations. Or certain actions may do the same, such as washing, anointing and breaking bread. The 'things' and the 'actions' are symbols of something greater than themselves, but even more than symbols, they may make God's presence and action so vividly alive and real to those encountering them in particular settings that they become sacramental. They become actual agents of change.

The Church of England defines this sacramental principle like this: a sacrament is an 'outward and visible sign of an inward and spiritual grace'. So the outward sign of baptism is water, and the inward grace is union with Christ in his death and resurrection, the forgiveness of sins and a new birth into God's family, the Church. The outward sign of Holy Communion is bread and wine. The inward grace is the Body and Blood of Christ.

> I am the
> Bread of Life.

Pushing further still, it's clear that nature can take on a sacramental reality. 'Earth's crammed with heaven, and every common bush afire with God,' wrote Elizabeth Barrett Browning. 'But only he who sees, takes off his shoes.' In other words, it's the coming together of the person, action or thing, with the recognition by the observer or participant, that causes the sacramental electricity to pass between them. That's when an object or action becomes sacramental.

> **In short**
> The sacramental principle is the idea that ordinary things can disclose the presence and action of God.

For discussion

- What might it mean that whoever comes to Christ will never be hungry?
- Can you think of occasions when a person, an action or a thing has taken on a sacramental meaning for you?
- How could you develop a sense of the sacramental identity of ordinary things?

How many sacraments are there?

This could get controversial!

The two chief sacraments of the Church are Baptism and the Eucharist. They're called 'dominical' sacraments because they are associated with the Lord himself (Latin *dominus*: lord, master). Baptism is the first step in a lifelong journey of discipleship, following Jesus day by day. The Eucharist is food for the journey and takes us closer to God.

However, Roman Catholics and some Anglicans refer to five other sacraments: reconciliation, confirmation, marriage, ordination and anointing of the sick. All of these can be channels of God's presence and action. In particular, many people have found that being anointed with oil when they have been ill has transformed their situation, whether in the spiritual resources they needed or in the actual state of their health. Similarly, the act of confession and absolution in the sacrament known as reconciliation has been found by many to be profoundly liberating, and many clergy lament the fact that the opportunity for such release is not taken up as often now as it used to be.

Two sacraments given us by Jesus himself and necessary for our Christian life –

- **Baptism**
- **Holy Communion**

Five sacramental ministries of grace that have developed in the Church to help us in our discipleship and mark some of life's most important moments with rites of passage –

- **Confirmation** – to make a mature commitment of faith
- **Reconciliation** – to assure us personally of God's forgiveness of our sins
- **Anointing of the sick** – to offer God's healing, strengthening and transformation during times of illness and at life's end
- **Marriage** – for the joining together of a man and woman in a lifelong covenant, the two becoming one flesh
- **Ordination** – the three historic orders of bishop, priest and deacon that developed in the earliest days of the Church's life and ensure that continuity of ministry and service between the Church in this age and the Church in every age.

Confirmation is also sacramental. This is how the Church of England defines it: 'It is the ministry by which through prayer and the laying on of hands by the Bishop, the Holy Spirit is received to complete what was begun in Baptism, and to give strength for the Christian life.'

Many of those who are discovering faith on the *Pilgrim* course will go on to Baptism and Confirmation, and then take their place around the table of the Lord. All that is required is a desire to know and receive Christ, penitence for our sins and a readiness to confess him as Saviour and obey him as Lord.

> **In short**
> There are two main sacraments, Baptism and Holy Communion, but there are five others that are also seen as channels of God's presence and action.

For discussion

- Returning to the stories we told each other at the beginning of the session about what worship means to us and the patterns we are developing, think about these other sacraments, the discipline of worship and how the sacramental life shapes and sustains our discipleship. What else do you need to think about? What questions do you have of each other's stories?
- If you haven't been baptized or confirmed, is this something you need to think about?
- What questions do you have?

Journeying On

Go on thinking about how the whole of your life can become a hymn of praise and an offering to God, and how worship, through a pattern of daily prayer and Bible reading, and participation in the worship of the Church, can shape your life. You may also care to look at ordinary things and actions and see how they might be vehicles through which you can see the presence and action of God. Start developing a discipline of looking back at the day's events, go through them slowly and try to pick out the moments when God has been visible in the things you've seen and done and the people you've met.

Concluding Prayers

**The cup of blessing that we bless,
is it not a sharing in the blood of Christ?
The bread that we break,
is it not a sharing in the body of Christ?
Because there is one bread,
we who are many are one body,
for we all partake of the one bread.**

1 CORINTHIANS 10.16–17

Merciful God
You have called us to your table
Generous God
You have fed us with the bread of life
Abundant God
**Draw us and all people to the service of your Son;
And send us out to bring your peace and goodness to the world.
Amen.**

Wisdom for the Journey

> You see on God's altar bread and a cup. That is what the evidence of your eyes tells you but your faith requires you to believe that the bread is the body of Christ and the cup the blood of Christ. These things are called sacraments because our eyes see in them one thing and our understanding another. Our eyes see a material reality; our understanding perceives its spiritual effect. If you want to know what the body of Christ is, you must listen to what the apostle Paul tells the faithful: 'Now you are the body of Christ, and individually you are members of it.' If that is so, it is the sacrament of yourselves that is placed on the Lord's table, and it is the sacrament of yourselves that you are receiving. You reply 'Amen' to what you are, and thereby agree that such you are. Be, then, a member of Christ's body, so that your 'Amen' may accord with the truth.
>
> AUGUSTINE (354–430)

Sacraments were instituted for the sake of sanctifying, as well as signifying.

PETER LOMBARD (1100-60)

As meat and drink do comfort the hungry body, so doth the death of Christ's body and the shedding of his blood comfort the soul, when she is after her sort hungry. There is no kind of meat that is comfortable to the soul, but only the death of Christ's blessed body; nor no kind of drink can quench her thirst, but only the blood-shedding of our Saviour Christ, which was shed for her offences.

THOMAS CRANMER (1489-1556)

Prayer the church's banquet, angel's age,
God's breath in man returning to his birth,
The soul in paraphrase, heart in pilgrimage,
The Christian plummet sounding heav'n and earth
Engine against th' Almighty, sinner's tow'r,
Reversed thunder, Christ-side-piercing spear,
The six-days world transposing in an hour,
A kind of tune, which all things hear and fear;
Softness, and peace, and joy, and love, and bliss,
Exalted manna, gladness of the best,
Heaven in ordinary, man well drest,
The milky way, the bird of Paradise,
Church-bells beyond the stars heard, the soul's blood,
The land of spices; something understood.

GEORGE HERBERT (1593-1633)

Our blessed saviour has set us the brightest pattern of every virtue, and the best thing we can do is form ourselves upon this most perfect example.

MARY ASTELL (1668-1731)

NOTES

Introduction to *The Eucharist*
[1] John Donne (1572–1631), *Divine Poems: On the Sacrament*.
[2] Augustine (354–430), *Commentary on Psalm 41*, 2.

Opening Prayers for all sessions
Common Worship, Times and Seasons, London, Church House Publishing, 2006, p. 520 and Lucien Deiss, *Biblical Prayers*, Chicago, World Library Publications, 1976, p. 52.

Concluding Prayers for all sessions
Common Worship, Times and Seasons, London, Church House Publishing, 2006, p. 520 and *New Patterns for Worship*, London, Church House Publishing, 2002, p. 299 (adapted).

Session One
Justin (died c.165), *First Apology*.
John Chrysostom (c.347–407), *Homilies on St Matthew's Gospel*, 50, 4.
Bernard of Clairvaux (1090–1153), *On the Love of God*, 7.
J. S. B. Monsell (1811–75)
William Temple (1881–1944), *Christian Faith and Life*, London, SCM Press, 1931, p. 18.

Session Two
Justin (died c.165), *First Apology*.
Hilary of Poitiers (315–67), *On the Trinity*, I.
Augustine (354–430), *Commentary on St John's Gospel*, 26, 13.
George Herbert (1593–1633), from 'The Agonie'.

Session Three
Irenaeus (130–c.200), *Against the Heresies*, IV, 18.
Clement of Alexandria (150–215), *The Teacher*, 1.6.
Cyril of Jerusalem (c.315–386), *Mystagogical Catecheses*, V, 21.
Gregory the Great (540–604), *Homily* 23.
George Herbert (1593–1633), *The Country Parson*, 22.
G. H. Bourne (1840–1925), 'Lord Enthroned in Heavenly Splendour'.
Anonymous (fourteenth century) *Anima Christi*.

Session Four
Anonymous, late first century, *Didache*, Ix, 4.
Augustine (354–430), *Sermon* 272.
Peter Chrysologus, fifth century.
Gregory the Great (540–604), *Homily* 23.

Session Five
Augustine (354–430), *Commentary on Psalm 41*, 2.
Evelyn Underhill (1875–1941), *Worship*, London, Nisbet & Co., 1936, p. 5.
Gregory Dix (1901–52), *The Shape of the Liturgy*, London, Dacre Press, 1945, p. 744.
Michael Ramsey (1904–88), *Be Still and Know: A Study in the Life of Prayer*, London, Collins, 1982, p. 123.

Session Six
Augustine (354–430), *Sermon* 272.
Peter Lombard (1100–60), *Sentences*, IV, 1.
Thomas Cranmer (1489–1556), *A Defence of the True and Catholic Doctrine of the Sacrament of the Body and Blood of our Saviour Christ*.
George Herbert (1593–1633), 'Prayer'.
Mary Astell (1668–1731), *The Christian Religion as Profess'd by a Daughter of the Church of England*, London, 1705, p. 158.

What's in This Pajama Party Book

A Note to Mom ♥ 4
Getting Serious with Pajama-Party Planning ♥ 5

Pajama Party #1
Princesses & Peasants
Have a Royal Ball! ♥ 7

Pajama Party #2
A Purple Pajama Party
Pass the Pillow! ♥ 17

Pajama Party #3
A Spa Party
Spin Your Nail Polish (Huh?) ♥ 35

Pajama Party #4
A Fashion Show
...Where You're the Model! ♥ 47

Dedicated to all the moms who sacrifice sleep
to let their girls have "sleep"-overs.

A note to mom

In recent years, slumber parties have come under the scrutiny of discerning moms. And for good reason: many times these parties are not well supervised, leaving the girls vulnerable to unfiltered Internet access and Netflix selections that you hope your daughter will never watch! (I write about this in more detail in my book *Six Ways to Keep the "Little" in Your Girl*.)

There are three reasonable responses to this.

One is to have a "no sleepover" policy. I've had friends adopt this, and their daughters survive quite well despite what everyone around them says.

The second is to let your daughter go to sleepovers only at homes where you know the family well and have confidence that what the girls will be doing is safe and morally appropriate. This policy is something I suggest you ease into when your daughter is 10, 11, or 12.

But I think the best option is to be the host home. This book makes that easy and sets you up to do just that, but even if you're a "no sleepover" mom, you can host a "pajama party." (Yep, I selected that title carefully.) And your younger daughters will love the thrill of having friends over in their jammies even if the party ends before the sunset.

Want to really up the ante? Invite the girls *and* their moms for some great girl gab! And enjoy your daughters!

Dannah

Getting Serious with Pajama-Party Planning

Is it possible to make your next pajama* party even more fun than the last one? You bet! You hold in your hands everything you need to host four of your own themed pajama parties.

There are two things that are going to make your parties different from all the rest: your mom and God. That's right—this is one slumber party with two special guests.

You'll enjoy some of the best-ever games, crafts, and recipes, but you'll also get cool, God-driven, Mom-directed story time and girl talk.

Now here's the thing: don't make your mom do all the work. Girl, this book has everything you need to get your party-planning skillz on! Here's your ultimate pajama-party-planning checklist:

One Month Out

1. Select a party plan. This book has four to choose from—Princesses and Peasants, the Purple Pajama Party, the Spa Party, and the Fashion Show. (If you want to do all of them, I suggest doing them in order.)

2. Write a list of friends to invite. Keep it small so you enjoy yourself. I recommend four to six friends.

---

* Just because you're in your jammies doesn't mean you have to sleep over. That's up to you!

3. Send out invitations. After your mom approves your list, send out invitations with the date, time, place, and a way for them to RSVP. (That's French for *répondez s'il vous plaît*, and it means "please respond." Don't ask me why we use French words on invitations. I don't know!)

One Week Out

1. Write it down. Since you might use my party ideas or add some of your own, you'll want to make a game plan. Putting it on paper ensures that you don't forget to buy something you need. What you write down should include your schedule (what happens and when it happens) and what items you need (basically your shopping list).

2. Go shopping. Ask your mom to take you to the store well in advance so you're not too tired to do all the work it'll take to pull off your shindig. (That's another one of those strange party words. It's not French, but it's odd!)

One Day Out

1. Bake, cook, organize, decorate. Do as much of this as you can at least a day in advance. It makes the day of the party easier, and you won't be too tired to host.

The Day Of

1. Have a pajama party. Enjoy!

Pajama Party #1

Princesses & Peasants
Have a Royal Ball!

Get your girly glam on with tiaras and all-things-pink, or roll it out medieval style with knights and castles. You choose how to theme and decorate your party. I'll give you all the snack recipes, games, and content that you need for a trip back to "once upon a time."

TRUE ... GIRL!
TG

Invitation Inspiration!

Use parchment paper to write a royal proclamation of festivities. Roll each invitation like a scroll and tie it with a ribbon. (Remember to tell your friends to wear their princess or peasant jammies if they want!)

wear your jammies!

8

Yummy Recipes!

True Girl Princess-Pink Popcorn

You'll need

- ♥ 4 large bags of popped corn
- ♥ 2 cups sugar
- ♥ 1/2 small box red Jell-O gelatin powder (you pick the flavor!)
- ♥ 1/2 cup water
- ♥ 1 tablespoon butter
- ♥ 1 teaspoon vanilla
- ♥ 1/4 teaspoon baking soda

Put the popped popcorn in a large bowl. Preheat the oven to 250 degrees. Line one or two rimmed baking sheets with foil.

In a medium saucepan (with room for the mixture to at least double in size), bring the sugar, Jell-O, water, and butter to a boil. Once the mixture is fully boiling, cook for 4 minutes without stirring, swirling the pan occasionally. Remove from the heat and stir in the vanilla and baking soda. Pour over the popcorn and toss with tongs to coat completely.

Spread out onto the baking sheets and bake, stirring once or twice, for an hour. Set aside to cool; break into chunks. Makes about 16 cups.

YUM!

YUM!

Princess- or Peasant-Themed Cookies

This one is both a recipe for yummy food and a craft to do at the party. Bake sugar cookies in a variety of shapes that fit your chosen theme. For a princess theme, you can make tiaras, glass slippers, scepters, ball gowns, and so on. For a peasant-themed party, you can make castles, crowns, shields, knights, and so on. Provide your guests with a variety of colored icings, small candies, and sprinkles. Let them decorate their cookies.

decorate some fun!

Scepter Berries

You'll need

- large strawberries with stems
- white chocolate (such as Nestle Premier White Morsels or Wilton White Candy Melts; 1 cup of pieces will coat about 12 strawberries)
- red food coloring
- decorating sugar (sprinkles also work well)

Rinse the berries, then pat them dry with paper towels. Place the white chocolate in a bowl and melt it in the microwave according to the package instructions. Stir in red food coloring until the chocolate is tinted pink (5 drops for 1 cup of chocolate). Dip each strawberry in the chocolate.

Have a Royal Ball

Okay, game time at this party is going to be a ball—a royal ball! (But in PJ's instead of gowns. Why not?)

You'll need

♥ balloons

♥ a royal scepter for each girl

Cover the floor of one room in balloons that you've blown up with regular air, not helium. Hand each girl a royal scepter. (You can buy these or make them as a craft at the party. Just use paper towel tubes, construction paper, glitter, and stickers for a fun project.) Play some fun—maybe princess- or knight-themed—music. You can make this a group challenge and just have everyone keep the balloons in the air until they're tired of it. Or, make it a contest and assign one balloon to each girl. When hers touches the ground, she's out. The last one with her balloon in the air is knighted or crowned princess!

Mom's Story Time

Ask your mom to read this to you and your friends. She's going to ask you to blow your "trumpets" every time she says the word *royal*. You should make your trumpet make this sound: **"da-da-taaaa!"** It makes the story very silly and much more fun to do it this way. Trust me!

You'll need
- this book
- a "trumpet" for each girl (could be a plastic trumpet or a kazoo—or just use your hands to make a pretend trumpet)

da-da-taaaaa!

There once was a Prince who was quite royal. (*Pause for* **"da-da-taaaa!"**) He lived in a glorious castle, which was also quite royal. (*Pause for* **"da-da-taaaa!"**) The castle was high on a mountaintop where birds sang. Rushing rivers raced down the mountainside below, which was covered in acres and acres of flowers.

Now the Prince had many, many servants and soldiers at his side. They were also quite royal! (*Pause for* **"da-da-taaaa!"**)

13

This Prince had everything! It was a wonderful life, and it was very royal! (*Pause for* **"da-da-taaaa!"**)

And yet each day he would take a walk along the mountain ridge, gazing down into the valley with one hope. The hope that he would catch a glimpse of one poor and simple maiden. You see, the Prince saw beyond the simplicity of this little maiden. He saw her beauty. In fact he was absolutely *enthralled* by how beautiful she was. Each day the Prince would return and gaze upon her beauty. He loved her. And he deeply desired to be loved by her in return.

The King was witness to all of this. He knew that, as things were, it was impossible for the Prince to be loved by the maiden. He knew, having much wisdom from his years as King, that it could never work—the Prince being so powerful and royal. *(Pause for "**da-da-taaaa!**")* And she, being so poor, and far, far away. He thought to himself, *If I command her to come to the castle, the Prince will always wonder, "Does she really love me or is she simply obeying me?"* Then the King thought, *If I send my horses and guards and soldiers and banners into her world in a grand procession, the Prince will always wonder, "Does she truly love me or is she simply afraid of me?"* After all, it was all so very royal. *(Pause for "**da-da-taaaa!**")*

The King pondered this at great length, until finally he had a magnificent idea and whispered it into the ear of his Son. Upon hearing the plan, the Prince was very burdened by the great risk of it all…but the thought of being loved by the maiden was worth any risk. The Prince bowed before the King. The King decreed that from here on his Son would not say anything or do anything that a Prince would say or do.

The Prince then took off his crown, his robes, and his princely garments. He instead put upon his body the clothes of his poorest servant. The Father and Son embraced, knowing they were to be separated while the Prince pursued his love. The once wealthy Prince would now go live in the peasant village as the poorest of the poor. And so, he went down into the village to be near the one who had captured his heart…to see if she would love him back.

The End.

Or is it? Of course, the story is hardly finished. But that's how it was written. To be an open-ended parable or story to get us thinking about something really important!

I've got news for you. That story is *real*. The King represents God the Father. The Prince represents Jesus. And the beautiful peasant girl is *you*. Psalm 45 is a wedding song, which Bible scholars believe portrays the love God has for us. In verse 11 He says, "Let the king be enthralled by your beauty." In verse 13, He actually calls you a princess. Here's how the verses go:

> "Let the king be enthralled by your beauty...all glorious is the princess within her chamber."
>
> Psalm 45:11a, 13a

Pillow Talk with Mom

Spend ten minutes discussing the story. What are the girls' favorite parts? How is the King like God? How is the Prince like Jesus? Why do you think the story ends with the Prince coming down from the mountaintop—and we don't know if the girl chooses to love him or not? (You might talk about how we have to choose to love Jesus.)

Note to Mom: This story adapts a widely used parable from Søren Kierkegaard's *Philosophical Fragments*.

Popcorn Prayer

Before the night ends, offer up some "popcorn prayers." Each girl quickly "pops up" one or two sentences to God.

Pajama Party #2

A Purple Pajama Party
Pass the Pillow!

This party is all about the pajamas…and the beloved color purple! Invite your friends to wear their fuzzy slippers and their footie jammies or their crazy colored socks with a pajama gown. Doesn't matter what kind of jammies, just so they're ready to celebrate girl-style!

TRUE GIRL! TG

Invitation Inspiration!

Make a super-cute purple pillow cover to send as an invitation to your friends!

You'll need

- 1 purple pillow cover for each girl (get them cheap at a dollar store!)
- 1 free downloadable True Girl Pillow Case art (from mytruegirl.com)
- 1 sheet of Avery iron-on transfer paper for each girl
- 1 safety pin for each girl
- 1 sheet of paper to write the details of the party
- purple pens

First, download your True Girl Pillow Case art and the instructions from my website. Go to mytruegirl.com and look for our downloads page. Click on it. Then, click on the book cover with the title *Talking With Your Daughter About Best Friends and Mean Girls*. When you get to the next page, scroll down until you see "True Girl Pillow Case Art." Download and print this onto Avery iron-on transfer papers. Using the instructions on your Avery iron-on packaging, create a pillow case for each girl you want to invite.

Use the purple pens to write out the details of your party (time, location, whatto bring and wear, RSVP info, and so on). Then use the safety pins to tack this to each of the pillow cases.

You can deliver the invitations in person or you can mail them, but if you mail them you'll need big padded mailing envelopes.

Yummy Recipes!

flurp! flurp! flurp!
We just LOVE to say flurp!

True Girl Purple Flurp

This recipe is featured in one of our True Girl fiction books, *Danika's Totally Terrible Toss*, and is something my mom invented!

You'll need
- ♥ 1 can of crushed pineapple
- ♥ 1 can of blueberry pie filling
- ♥ 1 can sweetened condensed milk
- ♥ 1 8-ounce tub of Cool Whip

Mix the three canned items together the night before your party and refrigerate them overnight.

Add the tub of Cool Whip right before you serve it to all your friends.

FLURP!

Purple Layer Cake

You'll need

- 1 package white cake mix
- red food coloring
- blue food coloring
- 1 tub of white cake icing

Mix the cake mix according to package directions. Divide it evenly into four bowls. Set one bowl aside because you're going to leave it white.

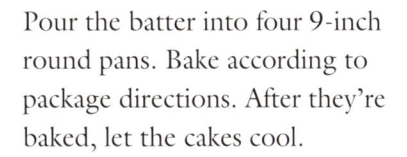

Add red and blue food coloring to the other three bowls, taking care to make one very dark purple, one medium purple, and one very light purple. This can be done simply by changing how much food coloring you use. Use more for a darker color. Use less for a lighter color.

Pour the batter into four 9-inch round pans. Bake according to package directions. After they're baked, let the cakes cool.

When they are room temperature, layer your cakes with white icing between them and then ice the entire cake in white. When your friends help you cut the cake, the inside is a wonderful world of purple surprise!

Frozen Grapes

You'll need

- 1 container of purple grapes

Rinse the grapes, then pat them dry with paper towels. Line a baking sheet with paper towels and place the grapes on top of the paper towels, leaving space between the grapes. Freeze overnight.

When you bite into them it's like a sweet, yummy grape sorbet! (Don't let them thaw out. They get real mushy!)

Freeze up some fun!

Pajama-Party Pillow Pass

Okay, game time at this party is super simple but lots of fun.

You'll need

- a pillow (and it'd be great if it's inside one of the purple pillow cases you made for invitations!)
- fun, upbeat music from your favorite Christian-music artist
- optional: purple candy

Pillow Pass is like "hot potato." Have all your friends sit in a circle. Assign one person to start and stop the music at random. (This person, as in all classic "hot-potato"-type games, can't look at the circle while the game is going on.) When the music starts, pass the pillow around the circle as fast as possible. When the music stops, the girl left holding the pillow is out (which means they become an official cheerleader for the remaining girls!). Play until there's a winner. (The winner gets purple candy.)

23

Guess Who?

This game should be played right before Mom's Story Time.

You'll need
- name tags
- purple markers

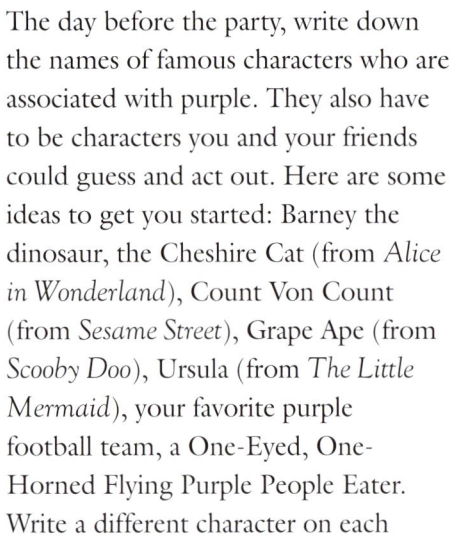

The day before the party, write down the names of famous characters who are associated with purple. They also have to be characters you and your friends could guess and act out. Here are some ideas to get you started: Barney the dinosaur, the Cheshire Cat (from *Alice in Wonderland*), Count Von Count (from *Sesame Street*), Grape Ape (from *Scooby Doo*), Ursula (from *The Little Mermaid*), your favorite purple football team, a One-Eyed, One-Horned Flying Purple People Eater. Write a different character on each name badge. (Make sure you have enough for everyone!) When it's time for the game, peel off the backing and stick a name badge on each guest's back. Have the girls mingle and try to find out who or what they're supposed to be based on how other guests socialize with them. Girls can ask "yes" or "no" questions to figure out what's written on their label.

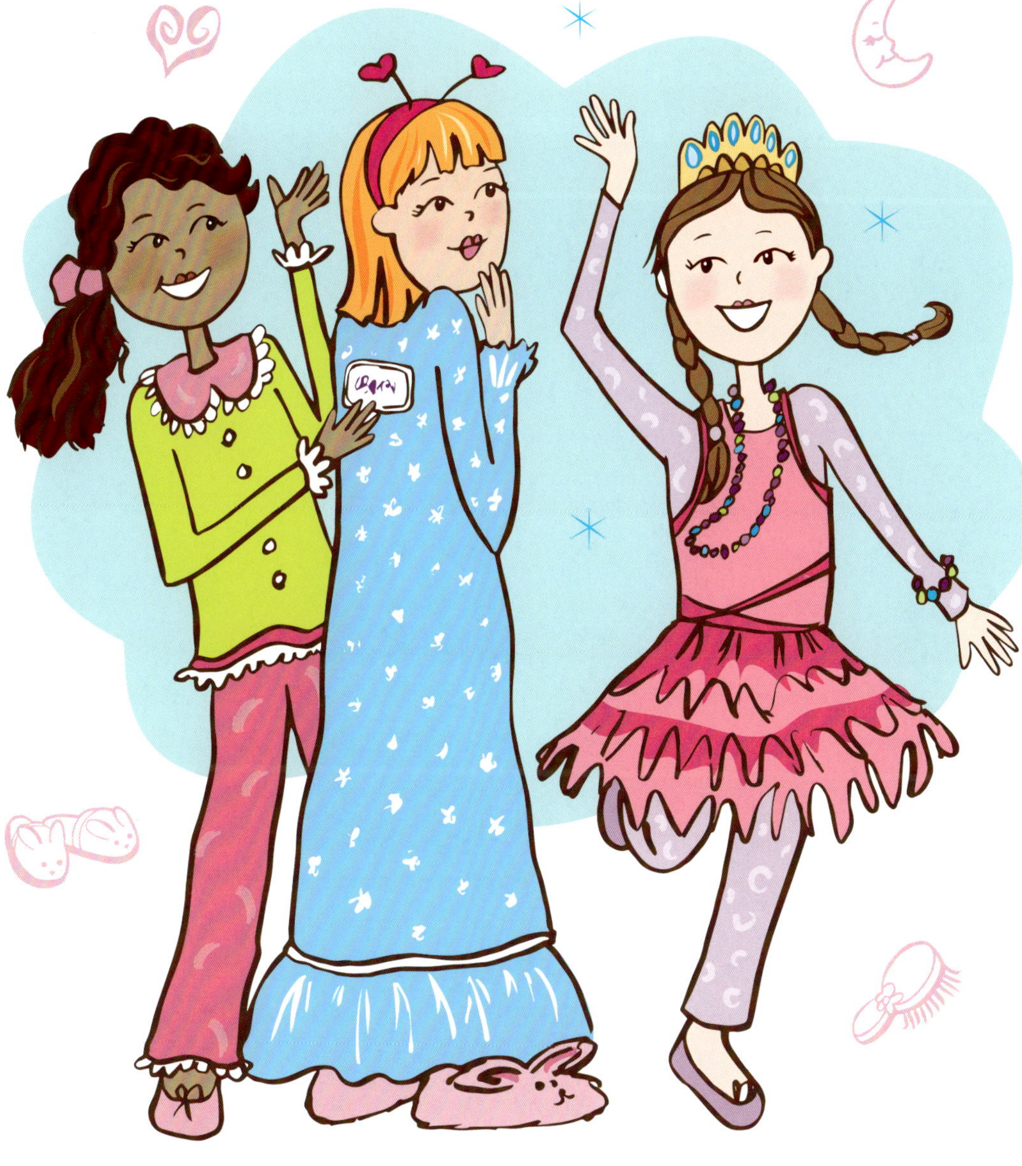

Mom's Story Time

Ask your mom to read this to you and your friends. Your mom is going to need to get her PJ's on for this great story. And she'll also need a few labels to put on them. You can help her by preparing these things.

You'll need

- this book
- pajamas for your mom
- six name-tag labels for your mom with these words on them: *ugly, unlovable, stupid, perfectly crafted!, loved by God!, empowered by God!*
- two blank name tags for every girl
- markers

(*Mom comes out wearing her pajamas and three labels on the front reading: "ugly," "unlovable," and "stupid."*)

Do you think my PJ's are funny? Ya know, a funny thing happened at some of the pajama parties I went to when I was your age. I came out looking…well, like this. Covered in "labels." Let me explain:

(*Mom should tell a brief personal testimony about her life. At some point it needs to tie into the labels on her. She can share about a time when she felt ugly, unlovable, or stupid.*)

she's smarter

she's prettier

she has more clothes

she's more fun

I want you to take a look around you right now. You will see girls you think are more beautiful than you, girls who look taller or smaller, girls who seem to be totally more confident than you… but here is the reality: every one of us has bad thoughts about ourselves. And if we think the same thing again and again, eventually we start to wear invisible labels. Maybe your label would be "unpopular" or "too tall."

I don't know what bad thoughts you have had about yourself, but I want you to know something: God is tickled silly pink, madly in love with you. Psalm 45:11 says, "Let the king be enthralled by your beauty." That's truth. Do you know how I know it is true and what you feel isn't true? Because the Bible says, "God is not a human that He should lie." But…here's the key…you have to be reading the Bible to recognize the difference between truth and lies. Let me show you how it works. The Bible says this in Psalm 139:14a:

"I praise you because I am fearfully and wonderfully made."

God is tickled silly pink, madly in love with you!

perfectly crafted!

God's Word says that every part of me is made wonderfully by God. That doesn't sound like "ugly" to me. No—

I'm "perfectly crafted"!...

(At this, Mom dramatically rips off "ugly" and replaces it with the label that reads "perfectly crafted!")

This lie says "unlovable." Let's see what God's truth says about that in Jeremiah 31:3b:

"I have loved you with an everlasting love; I have drawn you with unfailing kindness."

God *loves* me! His love is everlasting! I am lovable because God says so. **YOU are lovable because God says so**…(At this, Mom dramatically rips off "unlovable" to replace it with the label that reads "loved by God!")

loved by God!

Oh man, I am feeling free! Okay—one more label. Let's see. "Stupid." The bad word. The one we aren't really supposed to say. But I'm just saying it so we can learn. Hmmm. I have to say, I didn't get the *best* grades in my sixth-grade class (*or Mom says something truthful and similar*). How could God's Word answer that one? Let's look at 2 Corinthians 12:9:

"My grace is sufficient for you, for my power is made perfect in weakness."

Hmmm? What does this say about me feeling "stupid"? I think it means that I don't have to be the smartest girl in any class. In fact, when I am weak, God is strong. He'll use me no matter what. (*At this, Mom rips off "stupid" to replace it with the label that reads "empowered by God!"*)

empowered by God!

I'm free! Did you hear that? *Really* hear that? *You* are

- ♥ perfectly crafted!

- ♥ loved by God!

- ♥ empowered by God!

And that's just the *beginning* of God's thoughts about you recorded in the Bible!

Do you have any labels on you? Maybe you feel "fat" or "short" or like you have "no friends." Let me tell you something. Those labels are *lies*! And the only way to overcome them is to listen to *God's* thoughts about you as recorded in the Bible. Close your eyes and think hard. Ask yourself, **"What is my label?"**

I'm free!

FREE

Okay, if you have one I want you to come get one of these paper labels and write your "label" on it.

Just sit and wait there for a moment and really, really, really, really pray. Ask God to take this label…this lie… and rip it off you with his truth. I'm going to come read your label, and together we're going to see if we can find a Bible verse that says something more truthful about you.

hmmm…what is my label?

Pillow Talk with Mom

Spend ten minutes (or more if needed) helping the girls discover God's truth for them. As you do, take their bad label off and replace it with one that says something true. Then, talk about how everyone feels. Have you ever looked around at other people and thought they were better than you? Does anyone want to share what their bad label was and what their new truth is?

Note to Mom: We use this story in the True Girl Pajama Party Tour.

Popcorn Prayer

Before the night ends, offer up some "popcorn prayers." Each girl quickly "pops up" one or two sentences to God.

Pajama Party
#3

A Spa Party
Spin Your Nail Polish (Huh?)

This party involves fuzzy bathrobes and facials and manicures! But don't let the beauty treatments fool you—this party is all about making your inside beautiful!

TRUE ····· GIRL!

TG

Invitation Inspiration!

you are invited!

Use construction paper to cut out an eye-mask-shaped invitation (or buy cheap ones at a dollar store). Decorate the front to be cute and colorful and use the back to write out your invitation. Use a paper hole punch to put two holes on the opposite ends of the eye mask and put a string on it so your friends can bring it with them for an activity you'll do together. (Make sure you remind them on the invitation to bring their eye mask, wear fuzzy bathrobes, and bring one bottle of their favorite nail polish with them.)

Yummy Recipes!

(And since it's a spa party, all of these yummy treats are also healthy!)

Body-Cleansing Cucumber Water

This recipe and the Peach Facial below it are from my original True Girl resource, which is now titled 8 Great Dates for Moms & Daughters: How to Talk About Cool Fashion, True Beauty, and Dignity

You'll need

- 1 seedless cucumber, thinly sliced
- 1 pitcher of ice water

Soak the cucumbers in the pitcher of water for a few hours before you serve it. This releases the cucumber juice into the water. Serve in fun glasses with one cucumber slice on top!

Detoxing Colorful Fruit Kabobs

You'll need

- ♥ kabob skewers
- ♥ an assortment of firm, colorful, and easy-to-skewer fruit such as strawberries, pineapple chunks, mandarin-orange segments, green grapes, blueberries, black grapes, and so on (the berries will be what makes this a detox treatment that forces bad stuff out of your body)

Create a pattern of color from light to dark when you make your first kabob, such as yellow (pineapple), orange (mandarin segments), green (grapes), red (strawberry), blue (blueberries), and black (black grapes). Follow this pattern for all of the kabobs to give a dramatic effect on your party platter.

kabob! kabob! kabob!

38

Veggie Cups

You'll need

- 💗 cute mini-cups from a party store or dollar store
- 💗 an assortment of veggies cut into sticks, such as carrots, squash, celery, cucumbers, and zucchini
- 💗 a healthy veggie dip, like hummus, yogurt and dill, or anything else you enjoy that's healthy

Fill the bottom of each little cup with a couple of tablespoons of your favorite dip. Then stick the colorful veggies into the cup until it is packed full and looks adorable!

39

Peach Facial

I didn't know whether to put this under yummy foods or games, but since it's so delicious it ended up under recipes. Don't eat it all—it's for your face!

You'll need

- ♥ 1 medium peach per girl
- ♥ 1 tablespoon of cooked oatmeal with a little bit of honey per girl
- ♥ two cucumber slices per girl

(Important tip: Don't use this on the face of someone who has allergies to the ingredients. You can have a reaction even if you don't eat it.)

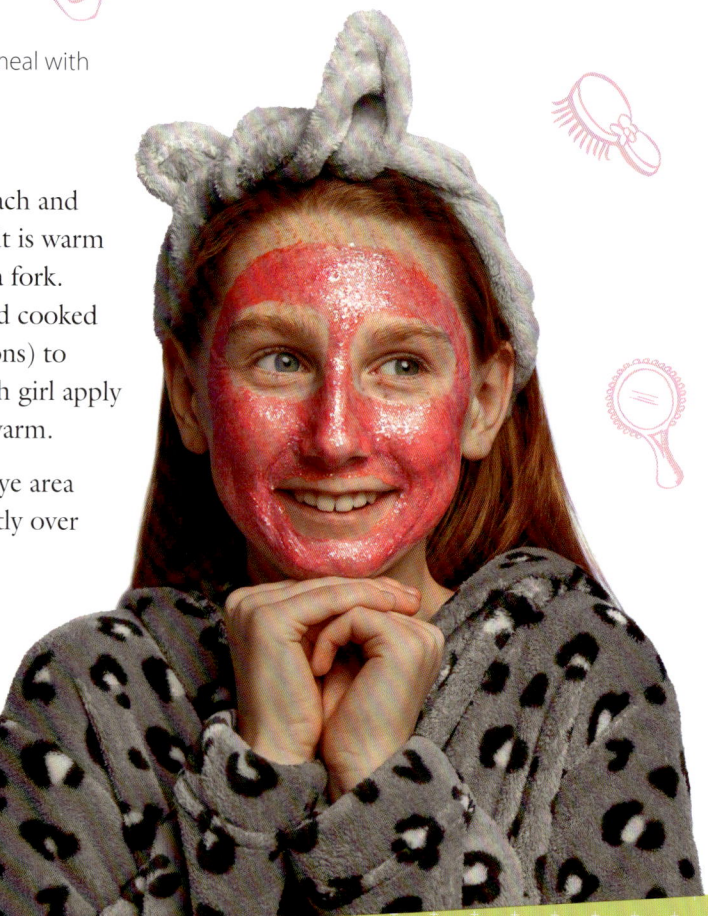

Take out the pit, peel the peach and cook it in a microwave until it is warm and soft. Then mash it with a fork. Add enough warm honey and cooked oatmeal (use package directions) to make a thick paste. Have each girl apply it to her skin while it is still warm.

Add cucumber slices to the eye area and place your eye mask lightly over them if you'd like.

Soak in the yummy aroma for ten minutes while you all listen to soothing spa music or nature sounds. Then rinse your face with cool water.

Spin

You'll need

♥ to ask each guest to bring a bottle of brightly colored nail polish

Each girl should have a bottle of nail polish. Have the girls make a circle and place their bottles in the middle of their group. Have the first girl spin a bottle of nail polish. Whoever the cap is pointing to when the bottle stops must paint one of her fingernails that color. Then that person spins the next color of nail polish …and so on. Pretty soon everyone has really crazy fingers and toes!

Celebrities Without Makeup

↳ **You'll need**

♥ pictures of celebs without makeup that you find online

♥ one sheet of paper and a pen for each girl

With your mom's permission or help, get on the Internet and look up photos of various celebrities without makeup! Celebs of any age are fine, but try to find teen and tween celebrities who usually wear a lot of makeup and don't always look the same without it.

During the party, show the pictures to your friends one by one without letting them see the name of the person and let them write down a guess. The person who gets the most correct is the winner. What better gift to give the winner of a spa-party game than a massage? No one to do it, you say? Well, what are friends for? Let each girl take a zone (head, shoulders, feet, hands) and give the winner the massage of her life!

Time

Ask your mom to read this to you and your friends.

I want you to know something. Every single face we just showed you is a masterpiece created by God. Especially without makeup. We carefully picked these particular stars to showcase because they are, in fact, especially beautiful.

But without their makeup they aren't very recognizable. And sadly, the beauty and fashion industry takes it even further. The photos of stars are altered and perfected using computer programs. Not only do these ladies have crazy amounts of makeup on, but most of the time their photos are digitally changed to impossible perfection.

every face a masterpiece!

So, what does the Bible say about your beauty? Well, it doesn't come from the paint in a makeup kit, that's for sure. How do I know? It says so in the Bible! Let me read you 1 Peter 3:3-4:

"Your beauty should not come from outward adornment, such as elaborate hairstyles and the wearing of gold jewelry or fine clothes. Rather, it should be that of your inner self, the unfading beauty of a gentle and quiet spirit, which is of great worth in God's sight."

Let me say this to you in conversational words. Your beauty won't come from a great haircut, some *fine* jewelry from Claire's, or a fantastic pair of jeans from American Eagle! Instead, it will show up if you work on making your heart beautiful by being quiet and gentle in the presence of God!

God wants you to feel beautiful. He doesn't say in this verse, "Oh, some of you might be obsessed with beauty and that's really a bummer. But oh…*okay*… here's how you get it!" Instead, God says "*your beauty*" as if it is a fact that you will and should have it! Two things about how you get it:

1 It's not that you can't have a really cute haircut, but that's not what is going to make you *feel* real beauty.

2 True beauty comes from quiet time spent with God. Period!

I have a question for you. Do you spend more time in front of the mirror each day getting your external beauty "on?" Or do you spend more time in quiet time with the Lord, getting your internal beauty "on?"

Today, I want you to make a promise, but only if you want to and really mean it. It's very simple.

"Today, I will spend more time in God's Word than I will in front of the mirror."

making our hearts beautiful!

Pillow Talk with Mom

Spend ten minutes helping the girls discuss how to have daily devotions. You can ask questions like, "Do some of you already read your Bible every day?" "When do you do it?" "Have you ever used a journal or diary to write your prayers to God?" "What are some other ways you can creatively pray?"

Popcorn Prayer

Before the night ends, offer up some "popcorn prayers." Each girl quickly "pops up" one or two sentences to God.

Pajama Party
#4

A Fashion Show
...Where You're the Model!

Come in your jammies, but leave in your favorite modest outfit!

TRUE GIRL! TG

Invitation Inspiration!

Go to a local dollar store and buy some funky fabric eyeglass cases. These are going to be your "sleeping bags" for the world's cutest invitations. (If you're really creative, you can sew your own mini sleeping bags.) Print out simple invitations with the details of your big party and slip them into the sleeping bags with the tops peeking out. They'll be extra cute if you can print little faces on the ends that are peeking out the top.

world's cutest invitations!

Key Verse

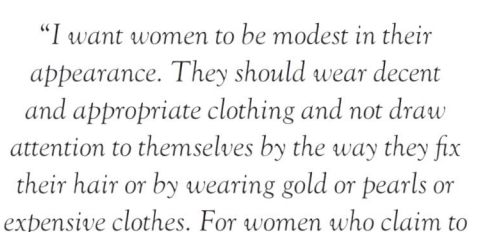

"I want women to be modest in their appearance. They should wear decent and appropriate clothing and not draw attention to themselves by the way they fix their hair or by wearing gold or pearls or expensive clothes. For women who claim to be devoted to God should make themselves attractive by the good things they do."

1 Timothy 2:9-10 (NLT)

Yummy Recipes!

Chocolate-Chip Cookie-Dough Dip

You'll need

- 1/4 cup soft butter
- 1/4 cup brown sugar
- 1 teaspoon vanilla
- 1 8-ounce tub spreadable cream cheese
- 1/4 cup powdered sugar
- 1 cup sour cream (optional)
- 1/2 cup mini chocolate chips
- sliced fruit and cookies for dipping

In a small saucepan, melt the butter and brown sugar and stir it until it's smooth. Remove it from the heat and add the vanilla. Let it cool.

When the mixture is room temperature, add the rest of the ingredients and mix it up until it's soft. Serve immediately or refrigerate. Serve it with sliced fruit and cookies for dipping.

Mini-Pizza Bar

You'll need

- 1 English muffin or bagel for each girl
- 1 jar of pizza sauce
- 1 bag of mozzarella cheese
- your favorite pizza toppings, like pepperoni, pineapple, ham, veggies, and more

This is a do-it-yourself snack. Each girl gets her own English muffin or bagel to cut in half and use to design her own mini pizzas. Just let everyone have fun creating, and then Mom can bake them all together at 350 degrees until the tops are warm and bubbly.

TP Fashion Designers

> **You'll need**
> ♥ toilet paper!

Divide group into two teams and give each team a roll of toilet paper. Let them pick models from their teams. Then give the teams two minutes to design an outfit using only toilet paper. Once two minutes are over, pick a winning fashion design and let the models strut the "runway."

51

Planning Your True Girl Fashion Show

Preselect

- 3 to 6 models of varying sizes (these should be the friends invited to your pajama party, because *everyone* is in on the runway action!)
- one outfit for each model (see "How to get the outfits" on next page)
- MC for fashion show (pick someone fun and outgoing)
- upbeat Christian music or music without lyrics with "runway" beat

How to pick your own fashion-show outfits. The goal is to use clothes that demonstrate "fashion problems" and show how to fix them emphasizing the True Girl "Truth or Bare" Fashion Tests (included in this chapter). Each outfit should be a different style (sporty, girly, etc…) to reflect the different tastes of the girl who is wearing it. You can write descriptions for each outfit to have read when the girl modeling it hits your homemade runway.

How to get the outfits. You can do this one of two ways. Go all out and buy or borrow an outfit for each girl, or ask each girl to use the guidelines in this chapter to create or find her own outfit. (You might assign one "Truth or Bare" Fashion Test to each girl. Although her outfit should pass all the tests, she can show how she had to be extra careful to not fail a test and what solution she offered!)

yeah shopping!

Ideas for problem areas to hit on.

- ♥ see-through blouse or open-knit sweater with a solid T-shirt or tank top underneath
- ♥ the trendy miniskirt paired with leggings or jeans
- ♥ a funky crop top partnered with a longer tank top in a complementary color
- ♥ a shorter shirt paired with high-rise jeans
- ♥ cool, trendy shorts with a 5-inch or 7-inch inseam
- ♥ a sweat suit without words across the bottom
- ♥ a shorter dress to go over jeans that are either skinny or too tight in the rear

Preparation and presentation.

Write up index cards with a description of each outfit. Get the girls all glammed up if you want. Then have the MC (one of the girls or your mom) get the girls all pumped up and in the right frame of mind to have a blast and clap and cheer for each other. Play the music and have the models come down the aisle one at a time as the MC reads the index card about each particular outfit. Encourage the models to have fun with spins and turns!

The "Truth or Bare" Fashion Tests

Finally, it's time for our nearly world-famous **"Truth or Bare" Fashion Tests!** Have the models fall into line on the stage. Have fun explaining each test. Have each of the models do the tests on themselves in front of the audience (the other girls), taking time to discuss possible remedies if an outfit doesn't quite pass one of the tests. For some of the tests, you can even have the audience participate. This should be fun—not shameful or embarassing.

TEST:
Raise & Praise

Target question: Am I showing too much belly?

Action: Stand straight up and pretend you're going for it in worship, and extend your arms in the air to God. Is this exposing a lot of belly?

Remedy: You can either make your shirt longer by adding a tank top underneath it, or you can make your pants taller by wearing high-rise jeans.

TEST:
Mirror Image

Target question:
How short is too short?

Action: Get in front of a full-length mirror. If you are in shorts, sit cross-legged. If you are in a skirt, sit in a chair with your legs crossed. Now, what do you see in that mirror? If you see undies or lots of thigh, your shorts or skirt is too short.

Remedy: If you don't want to wear something under your shorts or skirts, you'll need to buy some that aren't so short.

TEST:
I See London, I See France

Target question:
Can you see my underpants?

Action: Bend over and touch your knees. Have a friend look right at your bottom. Can she see the outline of your underpants or the seams in them? How about the color of them? Can she see your actual underwear because your pants are so low that you're risking a "plumber" exposure?

Remedy: Wear panties close to your skin tone with white clothes. If your pants are so tight that you can see the outline of your underwear, try buying one size larger or wearing a longer shirt to cover your bottom.

TEST:
Palm Pilot

Target question:
Is my shirt too low?

Action: Lay your palm flat on your chest with your pinkie and thumb about 5-6 inches apart. Is there skin still showing below your pinkie? OR lean forward a little bit. Can you see too much chest? If so, your shirt is too low.

Remedy: You'll either need to button your shirt up a little more or put something on underneath your shirt that has a higher neck so you can move around easily without showing too much.

Mom's Story Time

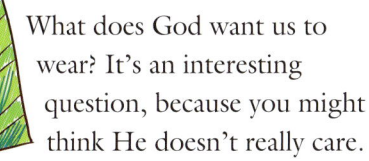

Ask your mom to read this to you and your friends.

What does God want us to wear? It's an interesting question, because you might think He doesn't really care. But the Bible says He does.

be a pet shelter friend!

Here's a Bible verse I like a lot:

"I want women to be modest in their appearance. They should wear decent and appropriate clothing and not draw attention to themselves by the way they fix their hair or by wearing gold or pearls or expensive clothes. For women who claim to be devoted to God should make themselves attractive by the good things they do."

1 Timothy 2:9-10 (NLT)

What God wants us to wear goes way deeper than jeans or graphic tees. He wants us to wear beautiful stuff *inside*. Our inner beauty are things like kindness, humility, joy, and helpfulness. And God-crazy girls wear these beautiful "garments."

God wants you and me to make ourselves attractive by the "good things" we do —like helping your grandma rake her yard or volunteering at a soup kitchen with your mom. I know a few God-crazy girls who are *beautiful* in this way. Like…(*Mom, insert stories about how the girls right in front of you have shown internal beauty. Maybe one of them has been a volunteer at a soup kitchen or another is a great big sister. Try to give an example of how each girl is beautiful.*)

*Y*ou wear beautiful stuff inside! God's ultimate purpose in 1 Timothy 2:9-10 is to push us into goodness, not to make a lot of rules about our clothes. Right?

But the passage does mention clothes. And it says they should be *appropriate*. Appropriate means "It's okay." Everyone say, "It's okay!" (*Girls say,* "It's okay!") So, let's see if some of these things are appropriate.

Is it OKAY to wear your swimming suit to church?

Naw! We'd look silly!

Is it OKAY to wear an itty-bitty skirt that shows your underwear when you bend over to help your friend pick up her books at school?

Naw! That's not okay!!

But every day the world is making it "normal" for you and me to be *inappropriate*. And it's not *okay. (Pause. Let it sink in.)* Of course, I haven't seen anyone wearing a bikini to worship, but I've seen plenty of short skirts at school! You know what I'm talking about?

I think the bottom line is this:

God wants nothing about the way we dress to distract from the good things we do for Him. That's why He wants us to be careful and modest about how we dress. That's why we like the famous "Truth or Bare" Fashion Tests. So you can know if an outfit is *okay*!

big sisters are cool!

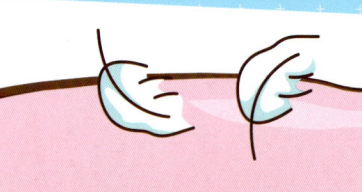

Pillow Talk with Mom

Spend ten minutes letting each girl share one thing that's beautiful on the *inside* of one of the other girls. Make it a true beauty time of encouragement.

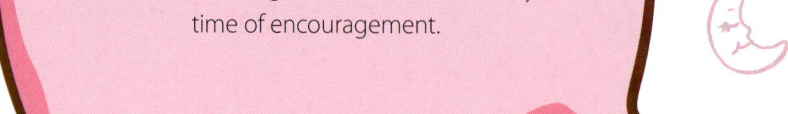

Popcorn Prayer

Before the night ends, offer up some "popcorn prayers." Each girl quickly "pops up" one or two sentences to God.

BIBLE STUDY TOOLS FOR GIRLS!

Meet the True Girl subscription BOX!

Packed full of things to connect you with your daughter as you both connect to the Lord!

DISCIPLE YOUR TWEEN WITH:

- Daily devos to get her in the Word!
- Mom+daughter dates that get you connecting!
- Carefully curated bonus items from True Girl and other ministries we trust!

Boxes are delivered every two months. Digital content arrives monthly! Digital only option available.

True Girl

mytruegirl.com/subscription